I Thought JESUS *Was a Swear Word*

Trudy Sherry and Carolyn Lawson

ISBN 978-1-0980-4426-8 (paperback)
ISBN 978-1-0980-4427-5 (digital)

Copyright © 2020 by Trudy Sherry and Carolyn Lawson

All rights reserved. No part of this publication may be reproduced, distributed, or transmitted in any form or by any means, including photocopying, recording, or other electronic or mechanical methods without the prior written permission of the publisher. For permission requests, solicit the publisher via the address below.

Christian Faith Publishing, Inc.
832 Park Avenue
Meadville, PA 16335
www.christianfaithpublishing.com

Printed in the United States of America

Thoughts about John 3:16 and Malachi 3:16:
For the book of remembrance was written about them who loved Him so much and who kept Him foremost in their thoughts… "And they shall be mine," says the Lord, in that day when I publicly declare them to be my treasure, my inheritance of jewels.

Then those who love the Lord talked often with one another about God and his doings.

I know the Lord listens in on some of my friends and I doing this.

Contents

Introduction: Kathleen Trimmer Ryan 7
Acknowledgements..9
Chapter 1:   Milk-Box Children 11
Chapter 2:   He's Alive! 13
Chapter 3:   Write the Vision 19
Chapter 4:   Fighting for His Life 23
Chapter 5:   Maybe I'm Not a Christian..33
Chapter 6:   Never Take Anything for Granted 41
Chapter 7:   The Rules of the Game..47
Chapter 8:   Basic Training...53
Chapter 9:   Miracles at the Detention Center 57
The Legacy Project 66
Chapter 10: A Deathbed Decision 94
Chapter 11: Miami Prayer Rally with Corrie Ten Boom 105
Chapter 12: Lord Teach Us to Pray 120
Chapter 13: Kidnapped and Left for Dead....................................124
Chapter 14: Lose Him and Let Him Go 131
Chapter 15: The Shepherd's Mark 133

Introduction

I can remember meeting Trudy and feeling there was something special about her—that I would like to get to know her better. Since that time, I have indeed gotten to know her, and she has been a positive influence in my life.

Several months ago, she asked if I would be interested in helping her by typing up a manuscript dealing with her experiences with the Lord working through her.

I had heard some of the stories, such as the one dealing with the healing of her infant son. Miracles can happen, and he is living proof of that. She had helped me deal with a *hate* situation that I was fighting toward a business associate and helped me overcome it… and get on with my life.

My *spiritual* life had consisted of going to church and Sunday school regularly with my husband and children, but as I think back, it was merely a routine playacting, thinking that if God saw us going to church, He would think we were good. But I had no spiritual connection with the Lord. I always knew He was there, but not for me in a personal way.

After moving to Florida about ten years ago, I did accept Jesus as my Savior and have had a sense of having a greater Being help guide me in my daily life. I've had some pretty rough times, but I always seemed to weather the storm through some miracle or other.

As I typed each chapter, I eagerly looked forward to the ending and had to control myself from reading ahead. I knew there would be happy endings—knowing Trudy and her ability to communicate with the Lord—but it was exciting to see just how each problem would be solved.

Trudy tells her story in a way that even the nonbeliever will have to stop for a minute and wonder what it is he or she is missing out on. It makes them realize that what is available to Trudy is available to anyone who wants it. They just have to ask.

Kathleen Trimmer Ryan

Editor's note: The skeleton of this book originated with Kathleen Trimmer Ryan. Years passed and when the time was right, new chapters were written and added.

Acknowledgements

The author would like to recognize and thank
Kathleen Trimmer Ryan
Carolyn Sherry Lawson and
Ann Marie Schell in the writing of this book.

Chapter 1

Milk-Box Children

Their faces seemed to stare at me from the milk box. Missing children…where were they? I tried to imagine if one of my own children were snatched from me. What would I feel like? Who could help me get them back?

I was a new Christian. So new, in fact, that I didn't know any better than to expect Jesus to listen to me when I prayed. I had not grown up in a Christian home. I came to Christ in my mid-thirties. The *older* Christians seem to speak a different language—words like redemption, sanctification, and intercession. I asked my neighbor—the pastor that prayed with me when my son was sick—what intercession was. He prayed, and God answered. My son was healed. Where did the power come from? Pastor Watson said it was when you intercede. It means you went to God on another's behalf. He said I could believe God would answer in Jesus's name according to his will.

This concept was new but exciting! The pictures of missing children on milk boxes and postcards were a means of alerting the public.

I started collecting the postcards. I looked at the children. Some of them seemed to draw me to them, like a magnet. I got a notebook and cut out the pictures that stood out to me.

I prayed constantly for each one. I prayed earnestly, night and day. The children became real to me. They were more than just pictures; they were children the Holy Spirit put very deep in my heart. I would pray for a hedge of protection around them. I prayed they would feel my love and concern when they were scared.

A year passed. I got the idea to call the National Center for Missing Children. I told them who I was, how I had been praying, and gave them my credentials so it would be a believable request.

She asked for each child's name—all twenty-six. We went through each of their stories.

Twenty-six children—fifteen rescued, one dead, one in prison, nine still missing. Never before had so many been found. He did hear me! It was a true answer to prayer. Intercession. I was a relatively new Christian. What other treasures did he have for me to discover?

Chapter 2

He's Alive!

> *"And when he had spoken these things, while they beheld, he was taken up; and a cloud received him out of their sight.*
> *And while they looked steadfastly toward heaven as he went up, behold, two men stood by them in while apparel"* (Acts 1:9–10).

"To become usable, you have to place a value on yourself. Most people have a low self-esteem, like you. You're not the only one. Just let go and realize you are a very special person. Accept yourself. Be yourself. Don't allow yourself to be controlled by others."

That's what my friend and prayer partner, Beverly, told me repeatedly in a hundred different ways. "But I can't do that by myself," I kept saying. "How can I be free of all the garbage?"

And there was so much of it! I was the middle child of a family of three daughters. My father was a rubber chemist and my mother had been a beautiful person, schoolteacher, and pianist. We lived in a gorgeous home on the *right side of town* and didn't want for anything…until I was five years old. Then my fairy tale life was shattered. My parents did what was unheard of at that time. They committed the *unforgivable sin*—they were divorced. To add to the trauma, my father left—moved away—and I felt utterly abandoned, totally rejected, as if in a whirlwind—every shred of security was suddenly, violently torn away. We moved out of our *castle* into a small rental house, and my mother got a job to support us. Attached to me now was the stigma of being a child of a divorcee…of the first divorcee in that small town back then. Everyone let us know it. People would change their path to walk on the other side of the street when they saw me coming. My sense of inferiority and my distrust of men began at that time.

Our first December in this new situation opened sadly. For two days my mother went around the house crying. When I asked what was wrong, she said, "There won't be any Christmas this year. Santa's not coming. We're not going to have any presents."

"No! No! Santa won't forget us!" I shouted. He couldn't. He was the one I had faith in. If he let us down, who was there left in the world to depend on?

Christmas morning, I rushed down the steps to see what he had left, while mother stood nervously on the stairs, bracing herself for the disappointment she knew was coming. But sure enough, there on the front porch were three stockings full of children's toys. "See, Santa didn't forget us!" was my triumphant shout. I didn't know it, but the neighborhood Presbyterian church had brought the gifts to us, although we had not gone there or into any other church for that matter. As I grew up, I did spend a lot of time in that church—in its basement which had a bowling alley. It didn't lead me to be a *good Christian*, but it sure did help me to become a very good bowler!

Each summer, we girls were shipped to an exclusive island off Long Island to be with my grandmother. I was torn between the two extreme lifestyles. I didn't fit in with all the wealthy kids living there. And as I grew older, I saw the masks people were wearing and couldn't talk to anyone honestly. But on that island, I began talking to God alone. All through my childhood, those *private conversations* were my only experience of faith.

When I was sixteen, I came home one night from my very first date and, to my horror, I found my mother passed out from the effects of alcohol. Many terrible things were said about my father that she had kept inside over the years. This, combined with loneliness and the burden of the heavy responsibility of raising three daughters alone, led her to becoming an alcoholic. This disease brought a complete physical and mental change in her which compounded all our other difficulties.

I was very confused and didn't know where to turn, so I turned to my newfound friend, John. He was different from the other boys. When he talked, I listened. He made history and government policies come alive. He seemed to know so much. He gave me the attention I craved, filling my need to be talked to. Most of the time we were at his house where his family got into intriguing conversations. Although his parents could only speak Russian, his sister and brother would switch back and forth to English so I could understand. We also went to meetings where I saw people from town that I knew and respected, so I figured it was okay. Other times we sat around his sister's kitchen table and I heard them talk about situations that baffled me. Their talk was about what was going to take place in Cuba and China and how this country was going to be infiltrated with their people who would work to carry out their goals of social revolution. Riots were going to be stirred up between blacks and whites, music to brainwash the youth would be introduced, priests and ministers committed to their cause were to be planted in the churches. They weren't afraid of religious people, only Christians. I didn't know what this all meant, but I loved the excitement of it all. And they accepted me because I was so close to their son. Some of the ideas I would question, but John explained them away until they made sense. I enjoyed being part of it all.

When we graduated from high school, John became a radio disc jockey, passing over the air many coded messages to others who were also working for the cause. I went to a small college which had granted me a physical education scholarship. It was the same town where my father and his wife lived and, for the first time since he left twelve years before, I lived in his house. After staying with him for six months, it was impossible for me to continue there so I returned home and entered the local medical center's school of x-ray technology.

I began talking a lot to a fellow student—the only boy I'd met whom I felt I could trust other than John. One night he arranged a babysitting job for me for one of the doctors, saying he would come to visit me after the children were in bed. He did that, and before I knew what was happening, he raped me. I was devastated, full of guilt, and too ashamed to tell anyone. My fear of men deepened and I had no other boyfriends until I graduated from the medical center.

John was the only *safe* man in my life, so I decided to go where he was working and get a job as a registered x-ray technician in a hospital in town near him. We planned to get married. As I was leaving my house in New Jersey to go to the airport, my grandmother looked at me and said, "He's a damn Communist!"

I was so shocked to hear her swear, and to cover my confusion, I snapped back, "So what's a Communist?" and stalked out of the house. But her statement never left me. It was like a warning signal because by this time I'd started turning against my family and the values of which the US stands for because of the subtle brainwashing received from John and his family.

I saw John only on Saturdays or an occasional day off, but was happily planning my wedding in my mind. One day, I went to visit him and found what appeared to be his having an affair with another girl. Once again, my life was shattered. I couldn't believe it. He had high and totally straight moral standards. And I knew the girl he was with and knew they hadn't been going together. That week, he moved and returned to New Jersey. Confused, I pinned the girl down about what had happened. She told me that his mother had been sent out to Ohio by the party to break us up. This girl had been hired as a *setup* to get me out of the picture. They were committed Communists, and they knew I would never be one of them. His *choice* was between me and the Party—and the Party allows no choices. I never became a Communist.

Once again, I was let down by a man. I struggled to work every day now, doing my best just to work my way toward a promotion and a solid career so I could be independent.

One night I was getting off work, a fellow coworker went with me to a coffee shop while he waited for his girlfriend to finish her job. They refused to serve him because he was black. I was furious and let them know, showing myself to be a *real troublemaker* for the hospital. The next day I was fired. This was the last straw. To add to my misery, it was Christmas—the season of hope and joy, of which I had neither. I felt like the little girl who long ago had been told there would be no presents this year. Except now, it was worse, for I had learned that there was no Santa Claus, no father, and no boyfriend to surprise me on Christmas morning with any kind of gift at all.

There was this guy named Hub who was looking for a ride to the East Coast for the holidays. There was no reason for me to stay in Ohio any longer, so I decided to return home, find John, and hear the truth from his own mouth. *I might as well take this guy along. He could help with the driving*, I thought. Wrong again! When I picked him up at his fraternity house, he had obviously been partying all night. He was in no condition to be behind the wheel. In addition, we were in the middle of a terrible snowstorm which made the trip a nightmare.

We arrived at my house at 3:00 a.m. My mother was up, anxiously waiting for our safe arrival. The first thing Hub did was to take a bottle out of his baggage and offer her a drink, endearing himself to her forever. Outraged, I screamed at him inside myself, *You don't offer an alcoholic a drink!*

Hub went home to New York, and I found John. He made it very clear that we were indeed finished. So when Hub called me for a date, I accepted. Meeting in New York City, we spent the night going from bar to bar, and by the time the evening, ended he was very tipsy.

The next morning, he called to apologize and begged me to go back to Ohio and have a New Year's Eve date. Going home was a mistake I realized at this point because my mother was impossible to live with as an alcoholic. I had to get out. There was a possibility of accepting another hospital job I'd been offered in Ohio before leaving. So I left and never looked back at this point.

I did get the new job and began seeing Hub. He was a business major in economics with a minor in psychology. He had a course in political science which included the study of Soviet affairs and Marxism. I wanted to learn all I could about the truth of Communism after what it had done to John and me.

Hub, being five years older than me, a strong, solid football player, outgoing, and social, was the security I needed as I started my new job and life. He was like the father figure I never had. I wasn't dating him; I was studying with him. He was my teacher, my friend, my big brother. But one night as we finished our lesson on Marxism and were talking about personal problems, Hub exclaimed, "Trudy, with your personality, people are always going to take advantage of you, especially men. You need someone to take care of you. I can do that. I want to marry you."

Chapter 3

Write the Vision

I was eight months pregnant, and every time I went to the doctor, he wasn't there. The different interns never checked me completely but just patted my arm, saying I was fine. "Try to lose some weight," one admonished briefly, sending me home to *wait it out.*

Soon after, Hub left early in the morning for a long day of business. I felt terrible and, except for the essential care of our daughter, I simply sat on the kitchen chair, not being able to move because of the excruciating backache that plagued me. Then I began bleeding, and frightened, called the doctor. "Get to the hospital. Right now. I'll meet you there!" he exclaimed. The urgency if his tone frightened me even more. I had no car, no husband to help, no one to take care of our daughter. Then I remembered a newfound friend down the street who I called. Of course, they would help!

The wife took me to the hospital, and the husband stayed with our daughter. On entering the emergency room, the staff took one look at me and immediately put me on a cart and ran down the hall, shouting, "She's delivering!" They gave me an injection then, and the next words I heard upon waking up were, "You have twins!"

Although a month premature and small, they assured me that my new twin sons were normal, and after a week or two in an incubator, they would be out of danger. Hub arrived later, surprised but delighted with his two sons.

It was 11:00 p.m., two nights after the birth, and I was lying in bed awake when suddenly I was infilled with a deep, overwhelming experience of love. There was a presence in the room. Immediately, a vivid impression entered my mind in the form of a gentle voice speaking. I listened in awe and *knew* what was impressed with overwhelming love and that I must act upon it. Covered as it was in a cloud of calm, I waited until the nurse came on her night rounds and then asked her, "Would you do me a favor? Please call the Ohio State Research Center and ask them to come down in the morning before 8:00 a.m. I want to sign some papers."

The nurse, thinking I'd been affected by the trauma of the births, reported my insistent request to the doctor. On returning, she said, "The doctor wants to know why you are talking this way."

"I'd like to donate these two children to the Ohio State Research Center because they are going to die soon."

"But why must they be here at eight in the morning?"

"Because they are not going to live much past that."

I could not tell them that a gentle, loving voice had told me all this, but somehow I spoke with such a conviction and surety that at 7:45 a.m. the next day, all the people necessary were there and I signed the papers, filled with peace—a peace I could not understand, knowing it was not of myself but of that presence of *God*.

At 9:04 a.m., the first little one dies, and his brother followed him at 9:20 a.m. Even then, amid the sadness and concern of the staff, I felt calm. The nurse came in and said, "Trudy, we're going to move you to a different floor while you recuperate. It will be easier for you to bear your loss that way—away from all the other new babies and mothers."

"No, no, don't do that. I'm enjoying hearing the other babies. Please, it's okay." I had worked in this hospital and knew many of the doctors and employees, and I had a very satisfying feeling by the knowledge that someday the physical members of their tiny bodies would help someone in need of answers.

One of the doctors I knew well from work could not understand my state of mind and thought I was suppressing grief. As my tranquil state continued, he became more concerned. "Trudy, you're not going to be taking a baby home. You've got to face reality," he reasoned with me.

"I know. I know they died, but I know that it's okay." I replied, amazed at my quiet confidence and composure. I peacefully returned home on Sunday, eager to go back to my small daughter. Hub, unable to face the emotional storm which would surely break out when I walked into the empty nursery I had prepared with such care, had invited my mother out to be there, too, as moral support.

As it turned out, they were the ones in need of solace. They comforted each other the only way they knew how—drinking their sorrow.

In her drunkenness, mother began sobbing as if she was the one who had just lost two babies at birth. Putting her arms around Hub, she hugged him, crying hysterically. He didn't know how to respond. After carrying on, she tried desperately to throw herself down the basement stairs, but Hub grabbed her and placed her on the sofa.

"Oh God!" I cried out. "There's got to be a better way of life than this!" Shocked, I went into the babies' to-be room and fell asleep on the bed across from the crib. Just before sunrise, I woke up and went back into the living room. There was my mother asleep on the couch; Hub was sprawled out in the big chair in front of the television which was still on. I looked at the darkness in that room and turned back into the bedroom, shaking from very deep within me, and I said again, "Oh, God, there's got to be another way of life!"

I shut the door and leaned against it. Suddenly, the room began to light up with a brilliant light. To the left of me, an image of a man began to form. He had a white robe on. I knew nothing of the Bible; didn't even own one nor did I know about Jesus. I did *know* that this had to be a God thing. In awe, I fell to my knees. Then I noticed two other figures to the right also dressed in white. Engulfed in a love which was so intense, tears began to stream down my cheeks and I whispered, "Who are you? What do you want?"

This man in the brilliant white robe, the light which now flooded the room emanating from his entire being, in the same gentle voice from the hospital, responded, "Now your life shall be lived for me." All I felt was extreme love and peace I had never felt before or be able to explain. After this illuminated person peacefully spoke to me, He was lifted and out through the two high windows up towards the clouds. I said to the other two men dressed in white, "Who is He, and where is He going?" All I felt was a penetrating love.

CHAPTER 4

Fighting for His Life

"Have not I commanded thee? Be strong and of a good courage; be not afraid, neither be thou dismayed; for the lord thy God is with thee withersoever thou goest" (Joshua 1:9).

Now my life shall be lived—for whom? I didn't know who He was, but He continued to surround me with a peace that passed all understanding. I tried to share this experience with Hub, but he dismissed it as an emotional reaction to the trauma of the twins' death. He thought I was *nutty*. Over the years, occasionally I tried to tell two different people who I trusted, but each time my mouth got like cotton and I literally was unable to say anything.

For a year I absolutely lived in a bubble of peace and expectation. I lived with an anticipation inside of me all the time, like a kid expecting Christmas. And then I was expecting another baby. He was healthy and active and very much alive. When our son was five years old, we moved to Florida because Hub had been offered a job there.

It was Easter of 1960 when we came to live in our home in Miami, Florida. Donald, our third child, was born soon after. Whoever would have guessed how God would use this small boy to bring a family into a personal relationship with Jesus Christ?

After moving to Miami, we became involved in the Easter Bowl held each year in the Orange Bowl as extras. In the Easter drama,

Hub played Caiaphas. I was in the crowd sitting on the ground. As the man who played the part of Jesus walked among the crowd, reciting the sermon on the mount, I remember thinking, *I wish I could have lived back in the time of that man.* That's how we thought of Him. He was a part of the past like any other historical figure.

"Mrs. Sherry, you might as well take Donald home with you. You can watch him there just as well as we can here." It was a serious blood disorder, incurable and very inconsistent.

It was May of 1963 when the doctors gave us the diagnosis—*idiopathic thrombocytopenia* or ITP. What did that mean? He had low platelets, therefore his blood had trouble clotting. Donald had been in a children's hospital for weeks, taken when he was sixteen months old. He began bleeding under the skin whenever he was touched. He developed bruises all over his body, but mostly on his legs and arms. He would bleed from his nose and his gums.

After setting up an emergency communication system with the police and completely lining his crib and playpen with foam rubber padding, we brought him home. I made a three-foot bird feeder to attract birds to our living room porch area where Donald could see them. Every kind of bird South Florida had to offer came to visit, even the parrots from the nearby Parrot Jungle. When our two older children swam in the pool, I would move Donald to where he could watch them.

After about two months, Donald's blood platelets were back to normal. We tried to treat him as any other little boy, but we knew the inconsistency of his disease. A year went by and he was four months past his second birthday. While giving him his bath, he suddenly slipped, striking his face on the faucet. He had hit the bone just below the left eye. We rushed him to the hospital emergency room. An eye doctor treated him and sent us home with a prescription to be filled.

I stopped by the drug store on the way home, having to force myself to walk inside the store. I thought it strange at the time but disregarded the signal to stop. I finally did go in and obtain the required medicine. Once home, I gave Donald the prescribed dosage. It wasn't until he began bleeding and those ugly bruises began appearing all over his body that I looked at the prescription. To my horror, the doctor had prescribed him an anticoagulant!

For the second time, Donald was rushed to the children's hospital. He was admitted with a blackball hemorrhage and bruising. Again, a critically low platelet count. He had also begun to bleed from the rectum. He was in bad shape, and I knew it.

A pastor and his wife came to the hospital but they just sat there. They couldn't seem to help at all. When I couldn't sit any longer, I got up to find a phone and called my mother. "Mom, what do you do when you have a child that could die?"

She answered, "I don't know, Trudy." She couldn't help me, either.

I went home. All I could do was walk around in circles. Finally, I cried out, "God, if you are God, help me!"

Our neighbor had recently given my daughter Carolyn a bible. I got it out and it fell open to Joshua. Joshua 1:9 seemed to jump right off the page to me. "Have I not commanded thee? Be strong and of good courage; be not afraid, neither be ye dismayed: for the Lord thy God is with you wherever you go."

Before this latest hospital stay, I had just finished Catherine Marshall's book Beyond Ourselves. How much did I want God to help me? Enough to pray the prayer of relinquishment which she had written about. I prayed it.

By morning, Donald's coloring and direction of his life were improved and under control. He had a four- or five-week hospital stay, and then another month and a half at home before his platelet count was back to normal again.

One Sunday morning, Hub was planning to take our other two children, Carolyn and Steve, fishing. That small voice inside me began impressing on my mind again, saying, "Go back to the church. Go back to church today." I was as insistent as the voice that we go so much to the displeasure of my husband, the fisherman. We dragged the kids to their Sunday school class, and we went to the first Bible study for adults in the church.

As we came into the chapel, the teacher, Pete Stephens, handed everyone a Bible; no one there brought one. He simply began reading the book of Acts, which gives a report of events. I thought it was a history lesson about how Jesus left this world and his disciples. In the first chapter is a description of his last moments before He ascended to heaven and the questions the disciples were asking Him. When he got to Act 1:9, the disciples watched Him get taken up into the clouds. Then the disciples noticed two men standing at the side dressed in white. When I heard these words, I went inside myself and thought, *Oh, my God, that was Jesus Christ I saw after the twins died. He's alive! He's alive!* Then I nudged my husband and repeated, "He really is alive. I saw Him and the two men dressed in white."

From then on, I wanted to know how to get to know Him. I kept going back to the study, but they didn't tell us how to know Him.

I was confined at home with Donald. So I started a neighborhood garden club. I wanted to learn about Florida's floral plant treasures and since I was so isolated I wanted to keep busy. The flowers and plants around the outside of our screened-in pool were just beginning to bloom when an idea came to mind. I called the electric company to find out if they would be interested in presenting an outdoor lighting program. They considered it since they were asked to put a lighting booklet together for Westinghouse and General Electric and worked out the details.

On April 14, 1965, the electric company representatives came to put on a unique program. There was to be a garden club meeting at my home, featuring an outdoor lighting effect and flower show. One of the representatives who came to set up the lights began talking with Donald who was already three years old. The electrician spoke differently from anyone I had ever heard before, not so much in the way he spoke but in his words. I said to him, "You know, this child has quite a story behind him."

I then proceeded to tell the man a little about Donald's history. His reply caught me off-guard, "You people are blessed to have a child like your son."

"That's an odd thing for you to say," I answered back. Josephine, who came each week to help me clean my house during Donald's illness, had also noticed and mentioned that he *talked different than the average man about God.* (I remember how she would sing about the Lord while she cleaned.) I didn't understand what that man meant when he stated that we were *being blessed.* But he said he would like to ask me something when the program was over.

The next day he was at our house again. This time he was removing the lights used the night before. Everyone else had left, but he sat in the shade under our tree in the center of the circular drive. September in Florida is still hot and humid, so I took him a glass of water. As I handed it to him, he asked me, "Have you ever thought of becoming a Christian?"

I looked at him and answered, "How? How do you become a Christian? I thought Jesus was a swear word," I replied.

"Mrs. Sherry," he began. "It's by faith in Jesus Christ by prayer."

I interrupted, saying, "I don't know how to pray, I just talk to God."

At this point, he took his Bible out and went over some scriptures:

> "For God so loved the world, that He gave his only begotten son, that whosoever believeth in Him should not perish, but have everlasting life."
>
> "The thief cometh not, but for to steal, and to kill, and to destroy: I am come that they might have life, and that they might have it more abundantly."
>
> "For all have sinned and come short of the glory of God."
>
> "For the wages of sin is death; but the gift of God is eternal life through Jesus Christ out Lord."
>
> "But God commendeth his love toward us, in that, while we were yet sinners, Christ died for us."

"Jesus saith unto him, I am the way, the truth, and the life: no man cometh unto the Father, but by me."

"But as many as received Him, to them gave He power to become the sons of God, even to them that believe on his name."

"For by the grace are you saved through faith; and that not of yourselves: it is the gift of God: not of works, lest any man should boast."

"Behold, I stand at the door and knock: if any man hears my voice, and open the door, I will come in to him, and will sup with him, and he with Me."

After he showed me these scriptures and told me Jesus was alive today and told me I could know Jesus personally, too, he prayed with me. I asked Jesus into my heart. As simple as that. Then the man left. I thought to myself, *Now what do I do?*

He said to me, "Mrs. Sherry, I'm a new Christian, and I asked the Lord to lead me to someone who was honestly searching for him. Yesterday, when I walked into your house, I knew you were the person I had asked God to take me to."

When Hub came home that afternoon, I told him about asking Jesus Christ into my life but he didn't understand what I meant. I couldn't find anyone who could tell me more about this Jesus. We found those who spoke about church programs and others who talked about Sunday school, but no one we asked could tell us about the reality of Jesus in our lives, our home, and our problems.

It was October 1966 that I took Carolyn's girl scout troop on an overnight camping trip. Donald had not had any recurrence of bleeding or bruising for well over a year, so I didn't think anything of leaving him alone with Hub. We stayed Friday night, and then came home late Saturday afternoon. It had been good to get away for a while. I dropped some of the girls off at their houses, but there were some whose parents weren't at home so I brought them home with me. Their parents could come for them there.

As I drive into our driveway, I could see Hub out mowing the lawn with Donald, four years old now, following behind him. I got out of the car, then realized what I was seeing. "My God, he's bruised all over and bleeding again!"

"I really didn't know what to do with him, and I knew you were on your way home," Hub countered.

There was no doubt that Donald's blood disorder, true to form, had flared up again without warning. So we loaded all the girl scouts into the car with Donald and went to Baptist Hospital. The girls waited in the lobby, while I got him admitted. The platelet count was taken immediately. Sunday morning the report showed critically low platelets again, but this time there was something else, too. The white cell count was just too high.

When I returned home, a friend was there. I went to find the medical book that a doctor I had once worked for had given me. We didn't have computers to use to search topics then. We just had books and according to that book, all his symptoms, which included a swollen spleen and his labs pointed to acute leukemia. If he had acute leukemia that meant he would die in ten days. I became nearly hysterical. It was then my friend spoke up, "What happened to all your faith, Trudy?"

Hub and I were beside ourselves with worry. We couldn't even talk with one another, so he finally went to bed. Out in our living room, I broke down and cried. Sometime between 11:00 Saturday night and 3:00 Sunday morning, sobbing, I said, "God, I don't know what it means to be a Christian. I don't know how to read the Bible. I don't know what to do." Still sobbing, I cried out, "What do you do when you have a child you think might die?"

I continued crying as a sense of pending loss struck and overwhelmed me. How long I remained in that near-panic state, I don't know. But as I quieted, I remembered I had been given a book called Absolute Surrender by Andrew Murray. I got up, trying to think where I had put it. I had never even opened it before this. I stretched out, and as I read this book, heaven became a real place to me. I knew then as a Christian I would be going there someday when God finished working through me.

As for Donald, I wanted what God wanted. If that meant God's will was to take out little boy to heaven, then it would be okay. I would have another one waiting for me there. So based on what I had learned about God from this book, I said, "Lord, if what you did years ago is true and really happened, if you are the same yesterday, today, and forever, use our lives to show your reality to other lives. Please touch my little boy's life. Heal him like you did when you walked on earth. I surrender to whatever your will is, Jesus."

There is a peace that passes all understanding, spoken of in the Bible. It is just that it's impossible to understand or to define but given freely. At that point the whole room began glowing, and I said, "You did hear me." I fell asleep with this peace.

When we arrived at the hospital that Sunday morning, the doctors and nurses were waiting for us. I asked them, "It's not leukemia?"

"No, but he will have to have major surgery this week. Removing the spleen is our only hope to reduce the seriousness of this illness. There is another problem, too."

I could tell that their nurses were having a hard time keeping Donald quiet. We had been through this problem each time he had to be in the hospital. "Donald is banging the sides of the crib for attention. You'll have to stay with him to keep him from doing more damage to himself."

That was exactly what I did. Our four-year-old had a lot of spunk and knew just how to get his way. It hadn't taken him long to connect hitting himself when he got bored to get attention. Wham, another black mark would appear, and the nurses would come running.

Pretty neat trick!

I was thanking God that He truly was with Donald and wherever I went, just as He had promised that night two years before while reading Joshua 1:9.

No more than an hour had passed on Wednesday, two days before his surgery on Friday, a man walked into the room. He told me he was a pastor who lived in our neighborhood, but I didn't really know him. My two other children knew him quite well because his children played with ours. He asked me if I minded if he prayed for Donald. I was overwhelmed because no one had ever asked me that before.

I said "Yes," adding "What do you want me to do?"

"Nothing. You don't do anything," he said, as he went over to the crib. He put his arm around Donald and prayed. "God, I ask that this be your will to heal this boy. I ask that you use his life and all the Sherrys' lives for your glory." With that, he left. Just as quickly as he had come, he was gone. He prayed nearly the same as I had prayed that Sunday night after talking to Jesus personally when the whole room glowed.

It was on this same eventful Wednesday in late afternoon at the hospital that the phone in Donald's room rang. On the other end of the line, one of the doctors was calling from the lab where they had been checking Donald's blood constantly, trying to get his body built up for the operation.

He said, "Are you sitting down?"

Not knowing what to expect, I answered, "No, but I can take anything now." But the doctor kept insisting I sit down, so I obeyed.

"Trudy, medically speaking, we have no idea what has happened except what we call an instantaneous remission. This child's blood has gone back to normal. We've cancelled surgery. You can take him home."

I was overwhelmed, saying, "Who is this Jesus Christ? What is this person? This is a miracle!"

"No, no, Trudy. It's only remission."

"No, he's been healed. I know he's healed."

I was hysterical with joy. I called Hub at work immediately.

"Hub! Donald is healed! We can take him home!" Hub was numb. So much had been happening so fast. Overwhelmed, he said, "I'll be right there!"

While waiting for him to come get us, I got Donald dressed. I was thinking, *Instantaneous remission…that's what they say when they don't have an answer to a miracle, I guess!*

Bringing Donald home was pure joy. I turned to watch this little four-year-old boy of ours bounce and tumble from one chair to another for an hour with no bruises and no bleeding!

I praise God even now for our neighbor Pastor Watson's obedience in coming to the hospital when the thought came to him about praying for our son. We weren't even a part of his church and I was a new and bewildered Christian. I now know we are all part of, not this man's church nor that man's church but the church of Jesus Christ, all Christians.

Truly, Jesus did come that I, Trudy Sherry, and Donald Sherry might not have life and have it more abundantly, not in a time passed but right now, today. Truly, Jesus commanded me, "Be strong and of good courage. Be not afraid, neither be dismayed. For the Lord your God is with you, Trudy, wherever you go."

And he was with Hub, too, if only Hub could believe it as I now did.

Donald was checked for two years. He has never had a reoccurrence. He graduated from Florida State. He remains active and healthy today.

Chapter 5

Maybe I'm Not a Christian

"Howbeit when he, the spirit of truth, is come, he will guide you into all the truth: for he shall not speak of himself; but whatsoever he shall hear, that shall he speak: and he will show your things to come" (Joshua 16:13)

"But the comforter, which is the Holy Ghost, whom the Father will send in my name, he shall teach you all things, and bring all things to your remembrance, whatsoever I have said unto you" (John 14:26).

November had been cool. Football season was bringing 1966 to a close. I was in the kitchen fixing supper when Hub came in from work. "Trudy," he called. "You won't believe what happened today!" Hub was president of the Kiwanis Club, and I knew they had a meeting. What I didn't know was what had taken place to bring our lives another step closer to this God we wanted so much to know about.

"We had some fellows come talk to us. One of them, Eddie, was with an organization called Campus Crusade for Christ International. Ever hear of it?"

Without waiting for my reply, he continued. "Two other fellows were with him—football players from the University of Miami. Do you know what they talked about?" Then, half thinking to himself, said, "Only God could do it. Get my attention, I mean, through a football player." Hub went to Ohio State University on a football scholarship, so I knew the meaning behind God's attention-getter.

Hub went on saying, "One fellow, a Rick, talked about how he knew Jesus Christ personally and told us how his life had been changed. Trudy, I was impressed. These guys were big, tough football jocks!"

Hub didn't say anything about going up to Eddie after that meeting and inviting him out to lunch the next time he was in town. He had done it for public relations only and figured Eddie would forget about it.

But Eddie did remember Hub's invitation.

On January 5, 1967, Eddie called to see if Hub could have lunch with him. Hub said it was impossible because he had two meetings he had to attend—one a luncheon meeting and another that afternoon. However, when God gets involved in the events of any given day, you can expect change. Within thirty minutes of Eddie's call, both meetings had been canceled. Hub was free to have lunch with Eddie.

Eddie was Jewish, but he had found Jesus as his Messiah and Lord. This simply made him what I was told is a *completed Jew*—no longer having to wait for his Messiah. Because of his background, Hub decided to take him to a Jewish restaurant where he had entertained many of his business acquaintances. When they arrived, it was already crowded with Jewish people.

As they waited for their order to arrive, Eddie began telling Hub about Jesus Christ. Now Hub was uncomfortable. Not only had Eddie unexpectedly taken him up on an invitation extended purely as a courtesy but now here they were, talking about Jesus Christ—in a Jewish restaurant, no less!

When the food arrived, Hub ate as quickly as possible. Once outside again, they drove back to the parking lot of Hub's office. There Hub started to get out of the car when Eddie stopped him and said point-blank, "Hub, I know God loves you. I want to ask you a question." Eddie paused to await Hub's response.

Getting a go-ahead, Eddie continued. "If you were to die and go to heaven, why do you think God would have to let you in?"

Hub answered rather haltingly, "I'm a good husband, a good father, a good provider, and I go to church!"

Eddie countered Hub's answer with, "According to the Word of God, he would ask, 'Hub, do you know my Son?'"

By this time, Hub was puzzled, so he said, "I don't understand what you are saying."

Eddie then said, "I'd never forgive myself if anything happened to you. If you were on your way home, had an accident, and got killed, I'd want to know you were going to heaven and that your whole family would be together someday. You really should decide and do it now. What do you have to lose if you pray this prayer with me?"

Hub could offer no argument, so he prayed with Eddie. "Lord Jesus, I need you. I open the door of my life and receive you as my Savior and Lord. Thank you for forgiving my sins. Take control of my life. Make me the kind of person you want me to be."

Hub now had become a Christian. It wasn't an easy time for him. He is an extremely intelligent businessman. He has superb reasoning power, and while this is an asset in the business world, it can become a stumbling block when learning to walk by faith in God.

Four months later Hub was in an automobile accident. It was a Friday night in May 1967. We had been at a bowling banquet and party. Hub had left the party to go home and check on the children. On the way back to the party, he blacked out, went off the road, and smacked into the side of a house. It was only by the grace of God that his life has been spared.

He was taken to the emergency room of the hospital where he had to have thirty-two stitches across his forehead. After he was treated, we took him home. I was completely discouraged and disgusted with him. Although Hub had stopped drinking, he had taken some drinks through a friend's influence. As it began to work in his body, the alcohol had thrown his body chemistry *out of whack*, causing him to black out.

God began dealing with him. He broke down and began to cry. He continued all that Friday night, all day Saturday, and into Sunday.

I went to our newly-found church alone; a church which taught about Jesus as a personal savior. A lady met me at the door. I guess with one look at me it wouldn't have been hard to figure something was wrong. I said, "My husband was in an accident Friday night." Since the service was beginning right then, she took me inside and sat with me. The sermon was about Peter denying Christ three times. The text was Mark 14:30–31, which said, "And Jesus said unto him, 'Verily, I say unto you, that this day, even in this night, before the cock crows twice you shall deny me three times.' But he (Peter) spoke more vehemently, 'If I should die with you, I will not deny you in any way.'"

When church was over, I turned to this girl and said, "Would you please tell Pastor Bob (the minister) of my husband's accident? Tell him also that I think Hub is denying Christ for the third time."

Because of his intellect, Hub was finding it very difficult to accept Donald's healing as from God. He looked at it as more of a coincidence. Now his life had been spared.

Just as I arrived home, our minister drove into the driveway. As he got out of the car, I went over to him and said, "Pastor, you can have him. After seeing miracles, healings, and becoming a Christian, now he's denying Christ. It's all more than I can take."

The pastor went inside and shared the person of the Holy Spirit with Hub. He said to him, "I think the only way you both are going to make it in your walk with Christ is by being empowered by the Holy Spirit. Look, there is going to be a lay institute for evangelism. You'll learn about the person of the Holy Spirit and how, with his power, you can live the Christian life."

He told us a little more about it. Thirty other people from church were going. It was to be at Tennessee's Lookout Mountain; the first such institute to be held in the southeast United States.

Because of all our expenses, hospitals, and doctors, Hub said no to going. But God wouldn't hear of it. A nurse from the hospital who had been taking care of Don when he was healed, Carol, came to my door and gave me an envelope. It had money from her tax return—the exact amount that we would pay for our trip to this conference. She also said her prayer partner worked in the same company and had been praying for us for two years.

Two weeks later, we were on our way with other members from this church. The first night they explained what would be taking place during the week we would be there, then to be ready for what God had to teach us. We had to *get straight* with God.

They said simply, "Get alone with the Lord and ask the Holy Spirit to reveal any sins in your life. As they come to mind, write them down on a piece of paper. When you finish, write across that paper the verse 1 John 1:9 which says, 'If we confess our sins, He is faithful and just to forgive our sins and to cleanse us from unrighteousness.' Then destroy the paper. Remember that God says He remembers them no more."

The following morning, I was overwhelmed with what I was hearing. They taught that the Holy Spirit was a person. They told us Jesus had to go away from the earth to send him. The Holy Spirit would come to us and enable us to live the Christian life. He would comfort, guide, edify, and instruct us in all truth.

Right then, as the man was speaking, I completely surrendered my life to Jesus. Truth—that is what I wanted. I wanted to trust in someone who could show me what was true and right. As I yielded myself, an incredible surge of energy and warmth went through my entire body. I realized fully that He would teach me all truth. I knew He would guide me and teach me how to pray. I needed to be comforted, and He would comfort.

I felt as if I had been hanging onto a raft going down rapids, struggling to keep a grip on something which seemed solid. Then, exhausted and unable to cling any longer, I let go. The sense of freedom and release relaxed me as I let go of the troubles I had been holding on to.

I began to cry, and my body began to tremble. I was unable to stop. Now there were 500 people there at that conference. I had never been surrounded by so many Christians before. They were all listening to the same message.

I had been concentrating my attention completely on the speaker up to the time the trembling began. Now I looked around me, but everyone was sitting quietly and listening. Everyone had seemed to be dry-eyed. I didn't understand. Why was I the only one there reacting this way? Not knowing what else to do, I got up and left to go to our room.

Hub came back to the room after the lecture and asked, "Trudy, what's wrong?"

After explaining what had happened, I said, "Maybe I'm not really a Christian. Why am I acting like this? No one else is."

Only God could speak through a new Christian such as Hub. He said. "Trudy, that's what we're here for! We came here to meet this Holy Spirit and to live the Christian life."

I hadn't realized that was what had taken place. Now I was excited. Of course! I had experienced God's power, had been empowered by the Holy Spirit, and now Jesus could live his life through me.

We learned much that week, and on the last day of the conference, we met with the group from home and prayed together out on the patio. We prayed for our homes and the city of Miami. We prayed that we would reach out and share our faith in Jesus.

As for me, I had become so involved in this attitude of prayer that I had become completely unconscious of the other people. Talking to Jesus alone, I prayed aloud publicly for the first time, asking God to forgive my involvement with my Communist boyfriend and allowing my mind to be brainwashed. "Thank you, Jesus, that you have sent me someone who will teach and guide me. Thank you, Jesus, that now you will be the one who will show me who is really trustworthy."

Afterward, one of the people in the group came to talk to me about my prayer and the mention of my *Communist boyfriend*, thinking I might be interested in an article concerning the severity and subtlety of what has been taking place in our country for decades.

These are the very topics I heard in John's friends' home, drinking coffee around a kitchen table.

Communist Goals to Fulfill the Rules of Revolution:

(Report uncovered in Germany in 1919)

A. Corrupt the young. Keep them away from religion. Get them interested in sex. Make them superficial. Destroy their ruggedness;
B. Get control of all means of publicity and thereby
   1. Get the people's minds off their government by focusing their attention on athletics, sexy books and plays, and other trivialities;
   2. Divide the people into hostile groups by constantly harping on controversial matters of no importance;
   3. Destroy the people's faith in their natural leaders by holding these latter up to ridicule;
   4. Always preach true democracy but seize power as fast and as ruthlessly as possible;
   5. By encouraging government extravagance, destroy its credit, produce fear of inflation with rising process and general discontent;
   6. Foment unnecessary strikes in vital industries, encourage civil disorders, and foster a lenient and soft attitude on the part of the government toward such disorders; and
   7. By special arguments, cause the breakdown of the old moral virtues: honesty, sobriety, continence, faith in the pledged word, and ruggedness.
C. Cause the registration of all firearms on some pretext, with a view of confiscating them and leaving the population helpless.

I returned home, empowered now to really live for him who had appeared to me in the light if his love so many years before. We were now empowered as a couple—or so I thought—and I took it for granted that our children now could catch *on fire,* just as I had. I could hardly wait to get home and fan the flames of faith. Then that voice buzzed quietly inside my head, "Trudy, don't take it for granted."

Chapter 6

Never Take Anything for Granted

> *"If we confess our sins, he is faithful and just to forgive us our sins, and to cleanse us from all unrighteousness" (1 John 1:9).*
>
> *"I can do all things through Christ who strengthens me" (Philippians 4:13).*

God said, "Never take anything for granted!" I looked at Steve, our middle child, sitting beside me in the car on our way home. Why was I so angry? No, not at Steve. He was only nine years old. Even before Donald was born, Steve had an extremely keyed-up nervous system. He was very hyperactive, and to compound the difficulty, he had a learning disability. When Donald had become so ill, Steve had gotten shoved to the sidelines.

We had spent the morning at the psychologist's office, and he had said nothing could be done to help him. That was what did it! I didn't believe *nothing could be done* for Steve. After all, we were Christians now—God can do anything! He had proved himself already. That's why I had walked out of the office with Steve.

For five miles, driving home, God's statement kept running through my mind. "Never take anything for granted!" I looked at Steve again and then I knew! "He's not a Christian!" My thoughts seemed to explode in sudden understanding.

I pulled off the road into one of the many little parks along the road I was on. They had been placed there to keep nature precious inside a big city. There was plenty of shade and even a cool breeze. I took a thin gold-colored booklet from my purse and began asking, "Steve, when you throw a ball up into the air, what happens?"

He answered, "It comes down."

"That's right," I said. "It's a law. A physical law. What goes up must come down."

Steve was listening as I continued, "There are spiritual laws, too. They could be called *facts*. One fact says that God loves you and has a plan for your life. Another fact reminds us that man is sinful and separated from God. This fact here," I said pointing at the place in the booklet, "tells you that Jesus Christ is God's only provision for man's sin. This one here," I said, as I turned the page, "tells us we must individually receive Jesus Christ into our lives. It is saying, Steve, that you are to ask Jesus into your life personally. Do you really want Jesus in your life?"

Steve looked at me and then at the booklet, asking, "Is it really that easy?"

"Yes," I answered. "That's all there is to do. Just ask Jesus in. But, Steve, you have to want him to come in."

Steve did ask Jesus into his heart. I started the car's engine. Again, we were on our way home. This time, though, I wasn't taking Steve's Christianity for granted!

Timmy, Steve's friend who lived next door to us, was in his yard playing. No sooner had the car come to a stop in the driveway than Steve bolted calling out to him, "Timmy! Timmy! I've had a new birthday! I'm a Christian! I'm like you. I'm a Christian!"

Timmy, Pastor Watson's was youngest son who lived in our neighborhood. Apparently, Timmy had been talking to Steve about being a Christian and being *reborn*. Now I knew even more surely that Steve understood what he had done.

A year had passed since that special day. It was now 1968. On this day, the neighborhood children crowded through the door, coming inside the house from playing football. Unscrambling the verbal chaos, it seemed that Steve, now ten years old, had been cussing, kicking, and bullying the younger players. The others walked out, leaving Steve angrily stalking around the living room. He was very hurt, very hostile, and very rebellious.

So far in my Christian life, I had learned to pray about everything and to rely on Jesus for answers. This was one of those times. I began to pray, "Lord, what do I do with this child?"

As the Lord gave me an answer gently in my mind, I looked at Steve, saying, "Steve, did you become a Christian because you knew I wanted you to or did you make your own decision?"

He answered me sharply, "No, I made my own decision." Then before I realized what was happening, he whirled around, angrily lashing out verbally, very loudly, and through clenched teeth, "You know what? I'm sick of being a Christian."

With all the frustration of a ten-year-old being let loose, he continued. "I try to be good and do the right things, like going to Sunday school and church. I try to listen and learn what they teach me, but it's too hard to be a Christian. I want to quit!"

I said, "Oh, dear God! Steve, please sit down."

As he reluctantly flopped hard into a nearby chair, the Holy Spirit began to reveal a story for me to tell Steve. "Do you know that little tree we planted in the front yard? The one inside the circular drive?" He gave me no response, except a look. "You know that in order for it to grow, it needs to be watered." He was quieting down and listening to me now, so I continued.

"How would you water that tree if all you had was the water faucet on the side of the house?"

He answered, "Well, I'd go over and turn on the water. I'd cup my hands like this and fill them up with water. Then I'd run over to the tree and dump the water on it."

"How long do you think that would last?" I asked. "Wouldn't you soon get tired and quit?"

"Well," he said slowly. "I guess I wouldn't last very long. I'd get tired." But then with new thought, he added, "Would the tree die, Mom?"

"No," I replied. "It won't die. It will rain occasionally, but the tree won't be a healthy one because it needs more water. Steve, suddenly you discover a garden hose under one of the bushed. It's available for you to use, so you do. You hook it up to the water faucet, turn on the water, and drag the end of the hose over to the tree. Because the hose is not clogged up, the water flows through it. Now you can give the tree plenty of water any time it needs it. You can water other trees, too."

Still watching Steve's reactions, I said, "Now listen really close. This faucet represents God or Jesus—the source of supply. Suppose you have two hoses to be hooked up to the faucet, if one is clogged with mud and the other is not, which one would you use?"

Steve answered, "The one that isn't clogged up."

"Don't you think the Lord should have that choice, too?" I asked. "Okay, let's say one of the hoses represents you and the tree represents other people. When you turn on the water and it flows freely, that's what Jesus talked about to the woman at the well as *living water*—his Holy Spirit. Steve, most Christians are so clogged up with their own thoughts, their own hates, disappointments, and garbage—their own sins—that they can't be available for God. He just can't work in and through them."

Steve asked, "How do I get unclogged?"

I drew a picture of the hose hooked up to the source of supply—the water faucet. When I finished the drawing, I said, "Now, let's go to the Bible to see what it says." I turned to 1 John 1:9 and read, "If we confess our sins, He is faithful and just to forgive us our sins, and to cleanse us from all unrighteousness."

Then I told him, "Take this pad with the picture of the hose and faucet. Go off by yourself. Either write down or put a little dot in the hose for everything that you know you have done wrong. Put down anything God would be grieved over. Anything He would call sin, even if it takes many pages."

When he came back a little while later, I saw that he had filled in the picture of the hose almost completely. Because of his learning disability, he had covered the hose with dots which was easier than struggling with the spelling out of words. Each of those dots represented to Steve all the things he had done wrong or which hurt God.

Seeing all those dots, I thought to myself, *Oh, dear! Has he done things I don't know about?* But I said aloud to him, "Steve, did you claim that promise in 1 John 1:9?"

He said he had.

"Then copy 1 John 1:9 from the Bible, writing it all over the sins on your paper."

I waited for him to write it out on the picture, then said, "Okay, now take your paper and rip it up in little pieces."

"Rip it up?" he asked, somewhat shocked.

"Yes, rip it up and go flush it down the toilet," I replied.

Puzzled, as any ten-year-old can be when his mother tells him to do something contrary to the usual, he said, "Okay, but why do I do all that?"

I explained, "Because that is what God said He would do if you confess your sins. He simply forgets about them. You gave them to him when you confessed them and wrote them down. They are no longer yours. You can't take them back if they have been flushed down the toilet."

When he came back from completing his task, I finished explaining. "Now you have an empty hose. It had better be filled with water or it's going to be filled with mud again."

Steve was quiet now, as I continued. "You are hooked up to your source of supply when you surrender and empty yourself of the garbage—the mud. Now what you do is say 'Okay, Lord, fill me up with your water.' This is what the Bible calls being baptized, submerged, or empowered by the Spirit."

That's exactly what Steve did. He asked for God to fill him up again. Then he asked me, "How about if I go out there and get mad at one of the kids again?"

I answered, "Then you had better get rid of your anger by turning it over to the Lord in a hurry or it will start clogging up the hose again! You have to want Jesus to take over."

For a time following our talk together, Steve would sometimes come in and say to me, "Oh, boy, my hose is getting clogged up again!"

I'd say to him, "Well, go! You know what to do with it. So do it!"

Steve now understood that what he said that one afternoon was true. There was no way he could live a Christian life and like it, unless he was constantly using the source of power Jesus makes available to him. As he claimed in 1 John 1:9, God would enable him to stay *unclogged* and available to be used as a vessel for God to work through.

Philippians 4:13 also became a powerful verse to Steve as it carried him through some rough places: "I can do all things through Christ who strengthens me."

The Lord has used this simple story many, many times. But there are two occasions which stand out vividly in my mind.

One occasion took place at a large Christian high school during graduation exercises. A teenager adapted this same story I had told her as the main theme of the commencement address she was to give. She had been impressed with the principles the Holy Spirit had revealed to her through it.

Chapter 7

The Rules of the Game

"For the Holy Spirit will teach you in that very hour what you ought to say" (Luke 12:12).

"What? Who, me? Why me?" I choked out. I had been standing in the courtyard of the church, drinking some punch that was being served. It was a beautiful April Sunday morning with all the foliage a bright new green. The pastor who helped me with Donald told us we could learn more about Jesus at this church, so we came and had been coming ever since. When Alice, Jane, and Bunnie came up to me after morning service, I didn't think anything out of the ordinary.

"Trudy, God has put your name on each of our hearts. We believe you are our answer to help us with the girls. Two weeks ago, we heard you tell us about Donald and how Jesus healed him. We heard the way you talked about Jesus answering specific prayers. You talk as if you have a special relationship with him. We want you to come tell the girls about him to teach them how they can know him like you do."

They explained what had been occurring. "Trudy, on our way home from the lay institute for evangelism, we began praying specifically for what each of us should do. Now we are teaching sewing to thirty-five girls living in cottages at a delinquent children's home."

With the necessary permission granted, the women set out once each week to Kendall Children's Home. Armed with the various materials needed for teaching the sewing classes, the women had already begun the work God had laid before them. "As we get to know each of the girls better, we share the good news of Jesus Christ with them. One by one, the girls have been asking Jesus personally into their lives. Now we want you, Trudy, to consider coming with us out to Kendall."

Taken rather by surprise, I answered, "I need to pray about this. I'll be back with you to let you know."

The Lord is ingenious about how He plants ideas—his ideas in our minds. I already knew a little about his technique. God's will begins when a seed thought is planted in your mind. As you talk to the Lord about it and let it rest awhile, you become assured it is Him. The secret of knowing if it is God's idea—right and perfect—or an idea from the enemy is the urgency factor. God never is in a hurry. Jesus never rushed anywhere. He never pushed the panic button. Satan, our enemy, always wants us to hurry, panic, rush, and do things without thinking. If an idea is from God, it grows and grows rather quietly and doesn't leave you.

My main argument was "But, God, I've never worked with or been involved with teenagers! I'm a Brownie and Girl Scout leader. I've never encountered delinquent young people!"

Carolyn, our eldest, was only fourteen then; Steve was eleven; and, Donald, seven. But God waited patiently for me to finish spouting all my arguments, then He sent through my mind, *Obedience, Trudy.* I had learned obedience. I knew what He expected from me. I wanted to please Him. I wanted to please my friend, Jesus, who had walked through so many difficult situations with me. I remembered all that He had done in my life up to this point. I was willing to do anything He asked. "Yes, Lord, I will go. I really want to learn all that you would have me learn and experience."

It was the week before Easter, the first time I drove onto the grounds of Kendall Children's Home. My first thoughts were, *How awful to be out here!* The grass, unshaded by trees, was already parched to a light tan color because of the absence of water. There was a suggestion of loneliness from the various buildings spread so far apart, with only one small swimming pool. The layout of everything placed on that land eliminated any feeling of coziness that the word *cottage* suggests. A feeling of solitary confinement struck me as I continued to drive through the ten-acre complex. The flat, barren acreage was broken only occasionally by clusters of gray-green scrub oaks.

I spotted the complex of cottages built low, seeming to hug the ground for security in the unprotected openness. The outside of the cottages were painted a light color, maybe a pale green. Although the air was humid and the temperature was in the high eighties, the look of coldness in the buildings sent a chill through me. Attached to the cottages were carports supported on round steel poles.

Inside the cottage designated for our use, I surveyed what I saw. The floors were light beige linoleum; the walls were painted cinder blocks, except for one wall completely windowed with *jealousie-styled* windows from ceiling to floor. Drapes had been drawn back to let in as much light as possible. The only furniture consisted of couches, chairs, and an upright piano. Today, metal chairs had been arranged in the huge thirty feet by forty feet room in two rows of semicircles.

The girls were seated in this semicircle, while the ladies from the church put on an Easter program. As I sat at the back of the room, all I could see were thirty-five girls filled with hate and bitterness. There was no unity. The girls seemed to be listening, but as I looked closely, I saw that their attention really wasn't on the story being told. It was as if they had flipped two switches—one to turn off the sound and one to turn on a *listening look*. The look so many teenagers are famous for—"Ho hum. Here we go again. I'm bored out of my mind. The same old stuff to listen to."

What they were hearing didn't mean anything to them. Why not? These girls had been involved in drugs, witchcraft, perversion, and even murder. There were girls from broken homes and were runaways. Just about everything the Bible warns us against doing, these girls had already experienced.

As I sat there, I really didn't know what I was going to say. I waited, saying to myself, "Hurry up, Holy Spirit. Tell me what to say. How can I reach this type of young person who has so many hurts?

They come from so many different backgrounds I don't understand and environments I can't relate to. Thank you, Jesus. You know!"

"For the Holy Spirit will teach you in that very hour what you ought to say" (Luke 12:12).

The story with flannel graph pictures was coming to an end. I still didn't know what I was going to say. Throughout the introduction, getting up, walking up to the front, still nothing came to me. I looked at the girls. Only I was standing before them this time. Again, all I saw was hate and bitterness. They were so different.

That was the key! Different! The Holy Spirit gave me the right words to say. Changing to a different type of story, I began talking with the girls. "Tell me. Suppose, after we finished here today, the administrator of Kendall came over. He would say to all of you, 'Okay, girls. Every one of you, I would like to know if you would like to be on an all-girls basketball team. If you do, there will be a bus leaving here at five o'clock to take you to Killian High. We will play basketball against their girls' team.'"

I had gotten the girls' attention. "Now you all know that Killian High is one of the roughest and toughest schools in the city right now, but you are so excited to be getting out of here that all of you show up at five. Here you are, getting on the bus, riding down to Killian High School. Once there, you each get a chance to play. Then the game is over."

Letting my eyes meet each of theirs for a moment, I said "Tell me. Who do you think won the basketball game?"

The girls were looking at each other. Suddenly, a very large girl said in a belligerent, sneering tone of voice, "We got beat!" It was as if she were saying in those three words, "Hey, lady. I know that school, who are you kidding!"

I quickly responded with "You had better believe it! You not only got beat, you got slaughtered! Why? Because, unless you know the rules of the game and have played it before, you can't play the game to win."

Watching them all closely, I continued. "Now some of you might know a little bit about the rules. Maybe some of you have even played a little bit. But you really didn't know the rules of the game.

The other team did. So you got slaughtered. Now this is the same thing with God. He created you, but He didn't leave you without the rules. Neither did He leave you without a rule book to show you what the rules are and how to play the game of life."

Then I said, "You know God has changed my life. I know there is another way to live. I know, too, that some of you girls are seventeen. You are going to be married in the next few years. What are you going to tell your kids? 'Come out here to Kendall Home. This is the way to live!' That's not real. That's not the answer. I've found out in my own life that there is another way. You don't have to live the way you are right now. You don't have to have only this as a way of life."

The girls were giving me their complete attention now. I knew they heard me and what was said *hit home*. What were they to tell their children?

With their heads full of new thoughts, I continued. "I want to share with you what's happened in my life. It's exciting! I want to show you how God loves you and how He has a plan for each one of your lives. If you really want to know why and how God loves you, the plan He has for your life, and about the power to live this life, come on Thursday and I will introduce you to the person who can show you how." (They didn't realize it was the Jesus in this *religious* story.) "But," adding firmly, "I don't want anybody to come because they have to. I want you to come because you want to find out."

With that last statement, I was finished. I think the girls and other women were as dumbfounded as I was. It was such a contrast, from a very religious story to kind of a crazy story or whatever you want to call it—*unorthodox*, the word might be.

I continued to share with these girls for three years. During that time, hundreds of girls became Christians. But while there, I came in contact with girls who had given their lives to Satan and were involved in occult worship. Many of them were lesbians as a result of the need for being loved. There were girls who had been raped; others had been sexually abused by their fathers. Some of the girls overdosed; some were involved in murders.

I had never come in contact with these things before. My answers came only as I sought the scriptures to learn how to deal with them. Because I didn't know anyone at the beginning who I could talk with about this, I turned to the scriptures, depending entirely on the Holy Spirit.

As I shared with these girls about the Holy Spirit, they were able to tell new girls coming into the home about the Jesus they had found. The girls were taught the basics of the Bible by women from the church who came once a week to the home. On Thursday of each week, different people from the various churches would come to give their testimonies. They brought their guitars and sang about unity that God wanted in his body of believers.

How would I come in contact with these people? I'd pray! Then as God would move, I'd either receive a phone call by someone passing through who would have something to share or I would arrive at Kendall to find someone already there waiting. They all would bring life and make Jesus real to the girls' lives. During the three years at Kendall Children's Home, a Thursday never went by that someone wasn't there with me. Through sharing, testimony, and singing, many revivals took place in individual lives.

Chapter 8

Basic Training

"Confess your faults one to another, and pray one for another, that you may be healed. The effectual fervent prayer of a righteous man avails much" (James 5:16).

The Thursday after Easter came rapidly. Here I was, Trudy Sherry, a brand-new inexperienced Christian coming to help others just as new in their walk with Jesus. At the lay institute, which Hub and I had attended earlier in the year, I learned to go to the Scriptures for answers. Upon returning, I knew I had to depend upon the Holy Spirit for my teaching ability.

Every girl returned to Kendall that Thursday, thirty-five in all. On the agenda was *getting terms understood.*

"Girls," I began. "In order for us to understand each other, I need to understand your language, and you will need to learn mine."

In this smaller room crammed with long folding-type tables and metal folding chairs, we had a *vocabulary day.* I had to learn to understand the *language of the street* in order to be able to teach them where they were right at that moment. The girls in turn had to understand basic words that I would be talking about.

I had invited some of the others to come out to help me, and together we took a survey on each of the girls. I wanted to know if any of them knew how to become a Christian, could they explain it to someone else, and if they knew who Jesus Christ was.

I found out from the survey that 95 percent of the girls had grown up with some type of church background. They knew the story of Jesus, they knew about Jesus, but they didn't know Jesus personally. So, as I was able to share Jesus as I knew Him, many of these girls, in addition to those who had prayed with the women teaching sewing, became Christians.

The next three years were to be my *basic training*. The time spent at Kendall Children's Home would give me the foundation in living a life of righteousness with the peace and joy of the Holy Spirit. I wanted these girls to see a relevant, alive Jesus.

"God," I prayed. "I can't relate with the street world these girls come from—this world of the occult and drugs!"

God seemed to say to me, "Trudy, you have My Son Jesus and you have My Power, the Holy Spirit. You will use My Rule Book. You will learn obedience and how to use the authority I have given to you."

I remember one illustration I used with this group.

"Girls, I have never understood the hymn *Onward Christian Soldiers* until just recently. Think of yourselves going into the armed services. You made a decision for Jesus. This is an army—a special one because God chose you especially to be in it. Not everyone is going to be in God's army, but now that you are a part of it, you learn He is boss, who the enemy is, what to expect from this enemy, how to defend yourself, and how to keep communication lines open. Basically, this last is learning how to pray—kind of a *walkie-talkie* type of practice."

Whatever I taught or explained to these girls, I had already experienced. In a sense, God would *walk me through* a lesson. Sometimes it was just the week before I was to pass it on. The experience was fresh, not only the victory in the outcome but the feelings and hindrances I came up against.

I didn't know there was a controversy as far as the gifts of the Holy Spirit go. Situations would arise I had never encountered before, so I simply had to depend upon the Holy Spirit to give the gifts He had promised. I used the gifts under his guidance because I didn't have the knowledge, wisdom, or the discernment naturally. I turned to the Scriptures, depending upon the Holy Spirit.

I viewed the gifts of the Holy Spirit quite like a plumber might view his tools. If you have a sink that is clogged up, you call a plumber. If this plumber shows up with a hammer in his hand, it doesn't take you long to decide that this man won't be of any use to you. You will say to him, "I don't need you!" You call another plumber who comes with his toolbox. He finds out what is wrong, then He uses the right tool that meets the need, clearing up the problem. His job completed, He continues on his way.

Joan's situation was just such a need. I needed some tools. Here was a young girl—a runaway with feelings locked up inside her. Of all the girls, Joan was the hardest to handle. She had run away from Kendall more than anyone else. Why did she behave in such an unruly manner? Memories buried, ugly memories that would bring guilt?

I spotted Joan one day walking slowly past the room where I was teaching the other girls. I caught her eye as she passed. I smiled at her. She must have stopped just outside the door because soon I was aware of someone half hiding, peeking her head through the door, trying to watch me. "Come on in," I called to her. She came in and sat down, but never said a word. She came three or four times after that. One day, about a month after my initial encounter with Joan, I received a call. "Mrs. Sherry, Joan's in lockup. Can you come?"

Lockup was a separate cottage. Joan had to stay there because she had run away again. Usually, the girls stayed at Kendall for about three months, but if their behavior was bad or if they ran away, they had to stay longer.

Driving out to Kendall, I prayed, "Lord, I don't know what to say to Joan. Give me your word of knowledge. I need your wisdom, also. I need to know how to impart this knowledge to her. Let her know that Jesus really loves her. Heal her life."

Upon my arriving, the housekeeper took me to Joan's room in the *lockup* cottage. It was like solitary confinement. There were bars on the window and on the door. I prayed again, "Lord, give me your word of knowledge." As I entered, she was staring at the floor, refusing to look at me. I said nothing but prayed until the Holy Spirit prompted me.

"Joan, you really don't want to go back home. You run away to stay here."

"Joan," I continued. "Jesus loves you and He will forgive you. He will also forgive your father. He wants you to forgive yourself."

Sending God a quick *Help*, I prayed, "God, what is the scripture?" I had borrowed one of the other girls' Bible since I had left mine in the car, and as I opened it, there was the scripture I needed! It had been underlined. "Thank you, Jesus," I breathed to him, as I read the verse aloud to Joan. "Admit your faults to one another and pray for each other so that you may be healed. The earnest prayer of a righteous man has great power and wonderful results."

As I finished reading, she began to sob. In broken sentences, she told me her memories, frustrations, and fears. "Every time I think about going back… If I go home, I can't stop thinking… My little brother died of leukemia. He was only five years old! I remember the day I watched my other baby brother choke to death. We couldn't do anything to help him! All this killed my mother. Then it was just me, my brother, and my father."

I found out that her father raped Joan. No matter how much she tried to love Jesus or to study and learn the Word of God, these memories would get in her way. Joan, as a Christian, had prayed to be empowered by the Holy Spirit, but he seemed to be blocked now because of the memories from her past.

"Joan," I said. "Right now, I don't know what the answer is for these memories. Will you trust me that as soon as I know for sure what to do, I'll share it with you? I'll be back Thursday."

She answered, "I trust you, Mrs. Sherry."

I had a week to come up with an answer. I went home. I grieved over the whole situation. I cried out, "God, there has to be an answer. What do you do with these memories? What do you do with damaged emotions?"

Chapter 9

Miracles at the Detention Center

"When Jesus saw that the people came running together, He rebuked the foul spirit saying unto him, you dumb and deaf spirit, I charge you, come out of him, and enter no more into him. And the spirit cried, and rent him sore, and came out of him: and he was as one dead; insomuch that many said, He is dead. But Jesus took him by the hand, and lifted him up; and he arose" (Mark 9:25–27).

The girls were literally banging their way into the room full of tables and chairs. One look at their faces and I knew trouble was brewing. But before I could think, a woman stormed in, pointing a finger and literally backing me into the wall.

"Mrs. Sherry, I know what you are doing out here. I will plead the First Amendment for these girls. I'm going to protect these girls' rights!"

She started giving me a rundown of her beliefs. As she was raving, I realized she had been under a very Communistic influence. With my past experience, it wasn't difficult to spot the *lingo*.

I had never met this woman but found out later she had volunteered to be a housemother part-time on a non-pay basis. Snapping sharply, she demanded, "What are these girls here for? Who are you? What right do you have to be here? I'll protect their rights!"

With me still backed into the corner of the room, this woman was verbally blasting away. The girls were standing in small groups, yelling to each other. "You told on me!" All around that room, hate twisted their faces, ready and willing to strike at anyone who cared to start a fight.

My thoughts cried out to God. *Lord, give me the knowledge of what you want me to say.*

His answer? "Just tell them about me!"

That is exactly what I did. As I began to speak, the girls began to listen. I told the woman how I knew Jesus and how my life had changed. I told her why I was out there. I didn't back down. I answered the woman's questions and accusations.

This volunteer worker backed down, turned around in an angry huff, and left. She walked out! The girls settled down somewhat after she was gone and that's when I found out about their *encounter group*.

For an hour before the girls would come to me, they would all meet in these groups held in the separate cottages. Their attendance was required. The idea behind the group was to confront the girls, bringing all the garbage in their past to the surface. The result? By the time they came to me, they were near explosion with hate, bitterness, and fighting. On this particular day, there had been a regular *girl fight*, complete with hair pulling. When these girls walked in, it was obvious that some of them had been crying.

They were still ventilating their indignities even now. "You told on me!" and "Squealer!" I couldn't get to the bottom of the real cause of the strife that afternoon.

As I left Kendall Children's Home, I prayed, "God, what has happened? What is causing this hate?"

I went to the Youth for Christ people (a national evangelical organization, who sponsored me, working with high school students in Miami). I asked, "Can you help me? I need to track down this hate situation in Kendall. I have to get to the bottom of this." I also asked them, "Is there anything you can do to get this woman who harassed me Thursday out of Kendall?" I explained the details.

They did help, and as a result, I had no more confrontations with the volunteer worker. But I still hadn't gotten any closer to the source of all the anger and hate. I prayed all week long. "Lord, reveal to me the root of the problem. Send me someone to let me know what it is."

The following Thursday, I arrived at Kendall. The girls began to come in one by one. Since their attendance was strictly voluntary, there was a more relaxed atmosphere. As some of them visited with one another, waiting for the others to arrive, a little Puerto Rican girl signaled for me to come to her.

When I reached the place where she was standing, she began saying, "Mrs. Sherry, I have to talk to you."

She was glancing around, obviously afraid of something. "I'm afraid they'll get me if they find out I squealed, but I have to tell someone. No one else knows what is going on here."

Still keeping her eyes on the others not far away, she stated, "They're fighting over what girl is going to be with what girl."

This girl was small, dark-skinned, with dark eyes and hair. She had every reason to fear. I understood completely as she unfolded the mystery of the hate. One particular girl was a lesbian—the leader. One by one, she had already gotten twelve of the thirty-five girls practicing lesbianism. What was happening? They were literally fighting for each other's love.

As I left Kendall that afternoon, I was praying differently. "God, I have never run into this before. What do I do with it?"

He answered. "Well, look in my rule book. Why don't you look in my Word?"

I turned to the Bible and there it all was, laid out for me exactly. I was ready for Thursday to arrive.

I went a little earlier in order to stop by to talk to the housemother who always came with the girls each Thursday. She had told me sometime before, "I'm a Christian. I'm praying for you."

Now I said okay. "I want you to pray for me very much. I'm going to say something I've never said before!"

When the girls came in, I had them sit down and allowed my eyes to look at each of them. All thirty-five girls were present. I began by saying, "I know what you all are doing. This is what God says about it."

Opening my Bible, I confronted the girls with the scripture passage from Romans 1:24–32 which reads, "Wherefore God also gave, them up to uncleanness through the lusts of their own hearts, to dishonor their own bodies between themselves: who changed the truth of God into a lie, and worshipped and served the creature more than the Creator, who is blessed forever. Amen. For this cause God gave them up into vile affections: for even their women did change the natural use into that which is against nature; and likewise also the men, leaving the natural use of the women, burned in their lust one toward another; men with men working that which is unseemly, and receiving in themselves that recompense of their error which was meet. And even as they did not like to retain God in their knowledge, God gave them over to a reprobate mind to do those things which are not convenient; Being filled with all unrighteousness, fornication, wickedness, covetousness, maliciousness; full of envy, murder, debate, deceit, malignity; whisperers, backbiters, haters of God, despiteful, proud, boasters, inventors of evil things, disobedient to parents, without understanding, covenant breakers, without natural affection, implacable, unmerciful; who knowing the judgment of God, that they which commit such things are worthy of death, not only do the same, but have pleasure in them that do them."

"Now, girls, knowing what God says, do you really want to live this way or do you want to go in another direction and be healed? If you continue to go in this direction, you will either stay the same or get worse. But you can be healed! Think about this."

After a week, the lesbian leader was transferred out of Kendall, although I had nothing to do with it. The move of perversion stopped, and I began once again to teach the girls. "Jesus is the one who can supply the love you are searching for. He will replace your loneliness with his special love."

This had been a victory only God could perform.

*****

Another situation involved a fifteen-year-old black girl, Alberta. Every time we said the name of Jesus Christ, she would yell, screaming out profanities and blasphemies. Continuing the disruption, she would sometimes throw her Bible across the room or would bring nude pictures of men with her to show around.

I didn't know what to do. I had also received a call from one of the women leading the Bible studies, asking, "Trudy, what do we do with her?"

I prayed, "Lord, what's wrong? What is the problem? Alberta belongs to you. You live in her heart. I know she wants you but, Lord, I don't understand her behavior!"

The next week at Kendall, a gentle, very feminine woman came over to me. She was one of the housemothers—a Christian. In her usual quiet manner, she asked, "Trudy, you know Alberta, don't you?" As I nodded, she continued talking, taking a paper out of an envelope. "She's written her mother a letter. I'd like you to read it."

Handing the letter to me, I read, "Mother, something happens to me every time I hear the woman who comes out here to teach us say the name of Jesus Christ. When I hear them use that name, something inside me goes berserk and I just want to scream. I feel like I'm being torn apart. I just rage inside of myself. Can you help me?"

When I looked up from reading the letter, the housemother told me, "Alberta's mother wrote back John 3:16, 'For God so loved the world that He gave His only begotten Son, that whosoever believes on Him shall have eternal life.' Alberta said to me, 'That's not the answer. I know Jesus is the only begotten Son. I understand that!'"

The housemother looked at me and said, "Trudy, I really think you would know what to do with this."

All I could think to say was, "Let me pray about it between now and next week."

That week, Hub and I were to go to a Youth for Christ dinner. We were sitting across from three of the men who were in leadership positions at the time—Gabe Domingus, Ted Place, and Jim Green. We all had known each other for a long time, so the dinner was spent sharing back and forth. Point-blank, I presented my problem with

Alberta. I said, "I know this has something to do with Satan, but I have never come upon anything like this before. What would you do?"

They looked at me, and Jim said, "What would Jesus do, Trudy?"

I answered, "I don't know, but I'll get my Bible out to see what He did do and just *do it!*"

At home, I read all the scriptures dealing with demon-possessed people. I made notes on how Jesus and his disciples responded to them. I realized I couldn't do this healing without help, so I got in touch with another woman who believed as I did—that if the New Testament said to do something, we were to do it! I asked her if she would go with me to the children's home. I asked, "Would you stand with me and pray with me while I talk with Alberta?"

She agreed, so the following day we arrived at Kendall. Driving just inside the grounds and under a good-sized grouping of shade trees, we stopped to pray. "Father, I plead the blood of Jesus to cover us. Protect us and our families."

The understanding and faith of a little child to do exactly what Jesus said was all I had. I believe strongly that God honors this childlike understanding and obedience of what scripture says to do.

This particular day, the women of the church were conducting their weekly Bible study. We had called Alberta to see us, and the three of us continued on to a small separate room—an unused bedroom off the main room. The lady I brought with me to pray took a seat in the only chair against the wall off to one side. Alberta and I sat on the bed by the solitary window. I began to explain, saying, "Alberta, your housemother asked me to come to see if I might be able to help you. I understand what is happening to you. Do you really want me to help you?"

Without hesitation, she answered a simple but very deliberate "Yes!"

I continued by saying, "Alberta, you either work for God or you work for Satan. I've been out here sharing the love Jesus has for you and about how your life might be changed. Remember the day I explained how you could become a part of God's army?"

She nodded without saying a word.

"Well, you have been in one army a long time. You had a lot of training and influence from the head of that army. It was an army of spirits. Spirits who tried in every way to destroy you emotionally and physically. But now you have changed into another army. As a result of having asked Jesus Christ into your life, the Father has given to you and me the authority to tell these evil, destroying spirits to get out. With these spirits gone, you will be able to worship Jesus the way you would like to worship Him."

I then asked her, "Alberta, is this what you are searching for? Do you really want to change over to God's army totally?"

Her reply was a short "Yes."

Explaining to her in more detail, I said, "I'm not going to talk or pray to God but rather I'm going to command. I'm going to be talking to the spirit within you. God has given me as a Christian the authority over evil spirits. It is the evil spirit that is causing you to react the way you do at the mention of the name Jesus Christ and when you are trying to learn more about God. Alberta, this commanding that we Christians are told to do is here in the scriptures in Mark 3:15." I showed her exactly where and placed a star beside it.

"Satan, in the name of Jesus Christ, I command you and all your spirits to get out of this girl. You are to leave her alone. You cannot go into anyone else!"

After thus commanding Satan to leave, we prayed with Alberta. I said to her, "I want you to pray and make certain you have invited Jesus into your life." I prayed first, using a simple prayer which she prayed after me. As she was getting up with her Bible in hand, I told her I would be back with her later.

As she was walking into the other room where a Bible study was in progress, I was saying, "Thank you, Jesus. Thank you for using me to bring someone life!"

Now Alberta had been under the care of most of the psychiatrists at a Miami hospital. She had been given drugs to calm her down while trying to get to this very fierce hate and anger within her.

Jesus took care of all that because she wanted him to! I didn't get to see her again because she was transferred out of Kendall soon after her deliverance, but I believed Jesus was working in her life.

*****

About a year after all this took place, another woman and I went to a conference in north Florida. It was to be the Narramore conference on Christian counseling. Hub and I and Bunny and her husband attended. The whole trip there, I had been sharing all the things I had been doing for and telling the girls about at Kendall.

Before our conference was to begin, we had understood that there was to be another conference taking place. The chaplains and administrators of all the penal institutions and state schools in the Southeast were attending. We wandered in and sat near the front. We were the only women there. The speaker announced a time of sharing of what had been happening at the various institutions.

All of a sudden, Bunny got up and began telling all that I had shared with her on our trip up from Miami. She told what had been going on out at Kendall. When the meeting was over, the chaplain of the Girl's State School of North Florida came up to us, asking, "May I have the materials you are working with that are being used? I want to put it into the state school." This was before Christian materials were not allowed in public institutions.

I found out through talking with him that he knew the material was effective because he saw the results. A lot of the girls from Kendall had been transferred to his state school. He was excited at the possibility of finding Christian resource material that communicated to these girls and brought results.

I needed encouragement in answering! "Of course! I would be glad to give them to you." I had prayed and wondered how the two could get together—the chaplains and the heads of the various institutions. Here now was my answer!

He then asked us both, "Would you come out and visit the school?"

Disappointed, I said, "I won't be able to. I'm to meet my husband at the airport."

Bunnie, however, was able to go. Later, when she returned, she exclaimed to me, "Trudy, you won't believe who was out there!" Without waiting for my answer, she said, terribly excited, "I went in and there was Alberta. The girl who was so viciously attacked and indwelt by Satan. Trudy, she has become a faithful Christian and has been helping the chaplain at the school!"

I knew God was faithful if we just claim his commands and promises. He is faithful as we obediently do what he says to do.

*****

It was now the end of 1971. The end of three years at Kendall. At this time, 2 Chronicles 7:14 kept coming to mind. It began to *grow on me,* morning, noon, and night, constantly running through my thoughts. As I studied it more and more, breaking it down, I found out that there were conditions we have to meet before God can fulfill his part.

It was becoming more apparent to me what was behind the home situations of these girls. I felt that if these young women would learn to pray and ask what God's purpose is for them, they would take their rightful place in the home. God can then bring unity. The young people would not have to find answers outside the home. I feel that most of the mothers are doing the best they know how, but they just don't know or understand how to find answers.

I was beginning to realize that my work at Kendall was finished. I knew he was taking me one step further into a ministry with these mothers. It has become a part of me to obey God. I knew it was God's will. I knew that the Lord wanted me to leave the work at the children's home.

The Legacy Project

As my mom approached her 90th birthday she said to me two months before, "I wonder if people will remember me like I am or like I used to be?"

The answer, of course, is both. I created a collage of pictures selected from the spectrum of my mom's life on one side of a card. The opposite side included an invitation to send me a story or letter describing how she had impacted their lives.

I sent out 90 cards. We received 86 replies! The following pages include some of the responses. My desire has been to bring her honor until she hears "Well done, good and faithful servant! You have been faithful over a few things, I will make you ruler over many things. Enter into the joy of your lord" (Matthew 25:23).

I THOUGHT JESUS WAS A SWEAR WORD

> Life is what we make it–
> and what a life you've made...
> Filled with friends
> and favorite memories,
> things you'd never trade.

Dearest Trudy,
Our rich and wonderful memories of you and your family trace back for nearly three decades! Throughout that time you have inspired us with your ministry of love and prayer. And you continue to inspire us today. In the love of Jesus, now and always. Thomas

> You see the good in others,
> and that colors all you do–
> For your wonderful example,
> here's to celebrating you!

Dear Trudy,
We do celebrate you and your legacy of love, your unwavering faith and your powerful prayer ministry. What a blessing you are to so many others, now and throughout the years! We are cheering for you as you celebrate 90 years with love, hugs and continued prayers. Jesu and Thomas

---

Over a month ago the Lord planted an idea in my mind. I had the enclosed cards made and sent out an invitation to 90 people to join me in what I am calling "The Legacy Project." As I have edited your book I have been inspired by not just your childlike faith but also by the way you have touched lives. I have never seen anyone share Jesus as much as you have over the years. How many people will be joining us in heaven because you have gently led them to our Savior. When you were so sick you said, "I hope people remember me. Not like this but for who I was." Get out the tissues and find out...

Little Momma,

**Today we're celebrating you
and all the lives you've touched...
We're celebrating
all the memories you've made
and the knowledge you've shared...
But mostly, we're celebrating
90 wonderful years of you.**

With a grateful heart,

The Legacy "C" Project is my gift to you for a life well lived →

TRUDY SHERRY AND CAROLYN LAWSON

GG,

I hope your birthday is filled with as much happiness, joy, and love as you are. How do I pick a favorite memory with you? Every time I see you we create new amazing memories together. I guess I will list a few of my favorite. First when we went to the beach and me and you walked arm and arm in the sand. Another is when you and Carolyn stayed at my house and you were there for my first cookout at my first house. I felt so much love in my home that day. I am so grateful I was able to come see you in August and earlier this November. Spending time with you is something I will always treasure. You also brought me much closer to the lord from writing your book. After I typed it I started praying much more. And let me tell you what has happened in the year since I typed your book. Stephen and I were so blessed to get pregnant with Selena after trying for two and a half years. We were financially blessed enough to pay off all of our debt. I was able to buy a brand new car, and we bought a home to raise Sophie and Selena in. I owe all of this to us typing your book and being much closer to our Lord and Savior. My last and

Celebrating
the amazing person you are
and the amazing person
you continue to become.

Happy Birthday

One of my most memorable memories with you is when you and Carolyn came to visit and you two prayed over me and I was saved. You are one amazing person and I will forever be grateful and blessed by the good Lord for you!

Love
Brooke ♡

Hi Trudy,
Here we are still sisters, alive & kicking. Happy Birthday from my heart - (bottom)
I'm sorry you & I have not been closer. Here we are, I think closer than we've ever been! You have been a truly loving sister for me - & for that I thank you - no words can express. Even though we're miles apart, you have been there for me!

Thank you too, being responsible for my asking Jesus into my heart! What would I have done these

Is that a lot of candles or is your cake on fire?

Happy Birthday

tough years without him? I hear a Big Amen to that also! Have a Great Birthday!
I love you dearly!
Alas, Fran (Snoonie)

I THOUGHT JESUS WAS A SWEAR WORD

Grandma,

Of all the memories we've made through the years one of my fondest is when we took a trip to Hawii. I remember the fire alarm going off in the hotel on our first night there! But the memory I hold on to the most, happened at the luau we attended. A question was asked, "Who has been together the longest?" You + Grandpa were pulled up on stage because you had been together for 50 years. That's over half a lifetime!
The love and dedication you had for each other is my inspiration for the loyalty I have with Erin.

Ninety is no ordinary birthday,
and yours is no ordinary life.

Happy 90th to the amazing,
the inspiring, the one-and-only you.

I hope you Have a wonderful day! Sorry we couldnt spent your special Day with you. But next year we will!
Love Josh

Trudy,
I am so thankful that god put you in my path when he did. I lost my sweet Mom in 2016. You seemed to fill that space in my heart. I love you and treasure your friendship. Lots of Love
Charell Dwyer

~ Psalm 118:24 ~
This is the day that the Lord has made. Let us rejoice and be glad...

Cindy Grubb © 2018

I THOUGHT JESUS WAS A SWEAR WORD

Nov 3, 2019

Dearest Trudy,

I hope this little note will bring you a Birthday Blessing!

I remember when I first met you I was at Sojourn church and you were still dividing your time between Highlands and Johnson City. Trudy - I believe your first name should be Encourager - or The Lighter! I so desired to get to know you, because of your enthusiasm and passion for God. It was probably a year later I met up with you again - this time at the Rock. Later I was invited to learn how to pray from you at Carolyn's house and I studied your materials, which helped strengthen my faith walk.

But when I think of you, I most remember the stories. The Stories of your faith journey. Stories of God visiting you in your home. Stories of God giving you Key direction, after →

you left your job as an X-ray tech. ~~the other~~ through verses you shared with me!

I've been so privileged to know you! The story of God healing your son, the story of Her leading you to lead the Florida prayer team. The story of meeting Corrie TenBoom and being transported! The story of God reaching out to the juvenile girls who were incarcerated - I soaked your stories in, because they weren't just about you alone - But they are God's stories and how amazing He is - and how He is working today still, even when we least expect it. I couldn't list all the God stories you told me!

Sometimes we walk through the valley - but we can look back and see how faithful He's been in the past and He will again. Thank you for sharing your life's story with me. I won't want to go back. I pray God will help you to continue to remember all He's done and know He's faithful to bring you safely to Home! Love, Suzy

71

TRUDY SHERRY AND CAROLYN LAWSON

Nov 8, 2019

Dear Trudy,

The first time we met was at "Pine Brook Worship Center." We had just moved into some apartments behind the church and you came over.

You noticed that I did not have many pictures and you offered to get me some. We looked through books together and you had everything I liked framed and you gave them to us! You were so kind and generous.

I later got to know Carolyn as we taught at the Christian school together where Megan + Micah became good friends.

Our families were beginning to get close to each other as I visited in your home in Highlands.

We had many wonderful times as we both loved Israel and talked about your time with Corrie ten Boom. You and I had so much in common and soon you were my prayer partner.

We moved to Jackson Hole, but you went with me in my heart. You were always there for me to call + know you would pray for me.

Trudy! You have always been there for me! You have encouraged me, promoted me to your friends, taken me out to celebrate my birthday. You have also been an encourager of all that Mike was teaching and a great help to me to get his CD's out.

You have always thought more of others than yourself. When you were going through

sad times, the death of Herb + Megan + your son, you were still asking if I was O.K. You are so self-less.

The fact that you always want more of Jesus no matter how old you get has inspired me. It would be so easy to think that you know enough now, but you keep seeking + studying. I want to be like you Aileen I am 90 in just 19 more years.

We will always share a love for Israel. Your "Shepard Music" have blessed many people and been a used to witness and I am so grateful for that.

Trudy, I love you. You are an inspiration and like a mother to me.

Happy 90 years young Birthday

Love,
Patty

I THOUGHT JESUS WAS A SWEAR WORD

November 8th '19

Dearest Trudy,

We've known each other over 55 years. I know because I was a young relatively new graduate from nursing school.

There are many stories, for knowing you then, almost daily, was such delightful Koinonia in our Lord - filled with nuggets and treasures; but my most favorite memory was meeting you in Baptist Hospital. I was taking care of a patient named Donald Derry, an adorable little towheaded guy. I was a fairly new Christian and so excited to have found our wonderful Lord. It did not take long for us to find our delight in HIM, together. Thus, began a lifelong sisterhood with you my precious friend who loved and heralded our Jesus everywhere. It was during the Jesus Movement, and heart, mind and soul, we together were part of that love affair with Jesus. We still are. That's why I chose this missionary. He's our Lord. We together, saw Donald Declad. And so much more. I love you. Blessed are. Carol Hamilton

---

Trudy,
Happy Birthday! You have truly served the Lord with your whole heart.
much love,
Melani Beavers

Dear Trudy,

You have been (and continue to be!!) such an example and inspiration to so many of us. Your joy, energy, dedication to prayer, and love for all has been remarkable and leaves a powerful legacy here at CBC and beyond. Praying that you'll be filled with happy memories and surrounded by love. We send our love and prayers.

Lisa (Bates) ☺

Trudy,
You remain a pillar in this ministry - you paved a way for many - Thank you for your prayer covering!
Shalom,
Cindy

Trudy!
We celebrate you, not just on this momentous birthday, but also for your faithful leadership, thankfulness and teaching over the past decades. And you continue to inspire us! Always in Christ!
Thomas

Trudy - You have been a blessing in my life and significant in the kindred faith family. You always bring joy to my life. I love you.
Theresa

TRUDY SHERRY AND CAROLYN LAWSON

Dear Trudy,
I am so thankful to know you. You are an example for me in your faithfulness, your love of Jesus, and your untiring efforts in bringing lost people into a relationship with Jesus!

What a great woman of God you are! A true princess warrior!

Onward Christian soldier
Marching as to war
With the cross of Jesus
Going on before!

✻

Each one should use whatever gift
he has received to serve others.
I PETER 4:10 NIV

I can't wait to read your book & get copies for my grandchildren. I want them to see what a life well lived looks like. You are awesome!!

Your willingness to use the gifts God has given you to serve is a wonderful blessing.

I love you with the love of the Lord!

John & Donnie

Happy Birthday!

Dear Trudy,
I can't believe that you are 90! What great memories of all those wonderful evenings spent at your house. You would fix us ham & roast beef sandwiches. (We only had bologna at our house! Ha Ha)

One of my favorite memories with you is 2 special nights of homecoming. (You let us borrow your VW bug and decorate it with crepe paper & chicken wire) You were right there helping us with it.

Thank you for all your prayers

We have everything we need to live a life that pleases God.
It was all given to us by God's own power, when we learned
that he had invited us to share in his wonderful goodness.
II PETER 1:3 ESV

for me & my family through the years.

Celebrating you
and praying your day
and the year ahead
are full of God's goodness
in every way.

Happy Birthday

Much love,
Bruce &
Jamie
Knight

I THOUGHT JESUS WAS A SWEAR WORD

Trudy,
What a blessing it is to call you friend. I will never forget two years ago when you joined us for Thanksgiving at mom's house. What a wonderful time it was! Happy Birthday to you, sweet friend. Much Love!
    Seth, Haley, & Lyla Bullock

Trudy —
Each time I open my Bible to the Psalms and see the note from you with scriptures of Psalm 51:11 and 51:17, I am reminded of the prayers and conversations we had as I walked through one of the darkest times in my life.

Words cannot express the gratitude for your prayers and encouragement during this time. Thank you for minding the gap for me and my family. Thank you for continuing to remind me that God is faithful and that He uses every piece of our brokenness to bring Him glory. This promise from Him has sustained me more times than I can remember.

I thank God for crossing our paths. Thank you for a lifetime of Kingdom work. I know God is pleased with your faithfulness to Him. Love you much.
    Shelly

TRUDY SHERRY AND CAROLYN LAWSON

Our lives are so wonderfully enriched from having you in them and your love, support, prayers and friendship are some of our greatest treasures in this life

When we count our blessing, and the things we treasure most, Trudy Storey is at the top of the list!

Please receive our love, honor, prayers and deepest THANKSGIVING for you on this special day — Love Always —

Mike Atkins

Dearest Trudy:

We are so thankful for the love & friendship we have shared together these many years! You are so dear to us and we so appreciate and celebrate you on this wonderful Birthday. You are 90 years young! You're youth is being renewed and you are so greatly loved and cherished — I pray that on this day you are able to understand, in part, just how much you mean to so many —

FROM MIKE ATKINS...

Happy & Blessed Birthday
TRUDY SHERRY!

HAPPY 90TH BIRTHDAY, TRUDY!!!

PLEASE FORGIVE MY TYPE WRITTEN LETTER FOR YOUR BIRTHDAY, TRUDY. I COULD TRY AND WRITE THIS BY HAND, BUT NO ONE COULD READ IT! HENCE, I AM TYPING.

I ASKED JESUS INTO MY HEART IN NOVEMBER OF 1967. I DO NOT KNOW THE DATE, AS I FELT THIS WAS NOT A BIG DECISION AT THAT TIME.

NOT LONG AFTER THIS DECISION, I MANAGED TO HOOK UP WITH TRUDY SHERRY! SHE AND HUB WERE FRIENDS OF MY PARENTS SOCIALLY AND THROUGH LON WORTH CROW.

I BEGAN GOING OVER TO TRUDY'S HOUSE, BLOWING CIGARETTE SMOKE IN HER FACE AND ASKING HER QUESTIONS ABOUT JESUS AND GOD AND THE BIBLE. I ASKED EVERY SINGLE QUESTION YOU COULD POSSIBLY IMAGINE. WHAT I REMEMBER MOST IS THAT TRUDY WOULD NOT ANSWER THE QUESTION, BUT RATHER SAY "LETS SEE WHAT GOD'S WORD HAS TO SAY ABOUT THIS SUBJECT". THEN SHE WOULD TURN SOMEWHERE IN HER BIBLE AND BEGIN TO ANSWER MY QUESTION USING A VERSE FROM HER BIBLE.

THIS LESSON WAS ONE OF THE MOST PROFOUND TRUTHS THAT TRUDY TAUGHT ME. <u>ALWAYS TURN TO GOD'S WORD TO FIND THE ANSWER TO YOUR QUESTIONS</u>. I HAVE BEEN DOING EXACTLY THAT FOR OVER 52 YEARS.

THANK YOU, TRUDY!

Casey

TRUDY SHERRY AND CAROLYN LAWSON

Dear Trudy, November 29, 2019

Happy Birthday! I am dating this letter for the day of your celebration, since Carolyn intends to give you a box full of these sentimentalities all at once. I hope you don't find it as overwhelming as I have. Given the fact that I write often, and edit even more often, I have found this assignment she gave us all to be one of the most overwhelming I've ever attempted. Mainly because I have so many memories crammed into what now seems to be a very brief ten or more years. I can't even remember exactly when we met.

What I do know is that I began my contract work at University Parkway Baptist Church in 2007, and by 2008 they voted me into full-time ministry. I do know that I was still finding my place there and had been assigned too many tasks to go into here, but more than once, those tasks crossed with your path at Parkway. One of them that I didn't much care for was the facilities. I had been told that I was the point person for the congregation, even though we had a maintenance guy, and Scott seemed to make most of the decisions anyway. We had discussed altering the side or back entrance more than once, and I believed I had provided the most reasonable cost effective solution, not to make a covered walk in the back, which was the only handicapped accessible entrance at that time, but instead to use the existing covered entrance at the side by simply altering the entrance walk there. We disagreed, and I couldn't understand why the sheer cost savings and quick solution was not agreeable with him. We had just had a conversation concerning this earlier that day, a Wednesday, when you pulled up to the side with Hub. Of course, there was no access to get him in, and it was raining. I think Scott and one of the deacons quickly assisted to get him up over the curb, but you didn't hesitate to give us all a piece of your mind concerning how ludicrous it was to have a covered drive to let people off and not have it handicapped accessible. I knew right then that you would be a great friend!

After that experience, I was afraid that you might not ever come back, but you did. I reached out to you, and by some miracle, and Carolyn's input too, I think, you returned. Another of my responsibilities in the church was the Adult Ministries. I had been discussing with Pastor Mike what I believed were the most important ministries in the church, with the Prayer Ministry being at the top of my list, and Men's Ministry a close second. He knew the current hand-full of ladies meeting on Wednesday nights was geared more toward the Billy Graham Telephone Ministry. We discussed making one of the classes that met on Wednesday evening about prayer. Well, you can't tell me that wasn't a God-thing when you met with him and told him about your Prayer Workshops! From then on, we began working together not just on your binders and brochures for the ministry, but also on the Shepherd's Mark. We were much more focused on your workshop in those early days, and I'll never forget telling Pastor Mike I was going to take you breakfast one morning and help a little bit with your binder, when we wound up spending the whole day working on it. I think he thought I was goofing off, ha, ha!

You impressed me so much when we first started working together, and it wasn't all because of your wonderful stories about your friendships with Vonette Bright or Corrie ten Boom, or even the supernatural stories of the Miami Prayer Rally and the unity that broke out amongst the Christians in different prayer groups as a result. It was because you inspired me with your deep passion to **teach others to teach** the Gospel story. This was when I began to find out more about the Shepherd's Mark and what your vision was. Your passion ignited a fire in me that has been burning closely to yours ever since! You and I have spent many hours pouring over the website, the booklet, the Facebook page, the oversized business cards, the cards for jewelry packets, the trademark, etc., etc. Not to mention the many conversations about meetings and the LLC, including onsite meetings and conference calls. And there is one thing that never ceases through it all, not only your continued passion, but also the loyalty of your friends and partners who have wanted nothing more than to see your vision for the Shepherd's Mark to be fulfilled, because we all share your passion for uniting Jews and Gentiles. This unity of both Old and New Testament believers is represented though your vision of the two triangles in the Shepherd's Mark centered around the gospel message of Christ's cross and the Holy Spirit's work in their lives. As we joined with you in this ministry, and I'm the newest on the scene, we all became deeply devoted, not just because we believe in the Shepherd's Mark, but because your passion for God's ministry in this is so inspiring to us.

2

TRUDY SHERRY AND CAROLYN LAWSON

Ann Marie

Beyond our devotion to the Shepherd's Mark, we are devoted to you Trudy. All of us have said at one time or another, that we were more devoted to you than to the cause. But you and the cause go hand in hand, because the Shepherd's Mark is just as much your legacy as your children and family are. It is this deep passion to see Jews and Gentiles united by Christ's sacrifice for us all . . . this deep passion that desires to see everyone saved. Your witnessing to complete strangers just for your love of Christ has motivated each one of us to press on. To keep the torch burning just as much for your sake as for the sake of all those lost souls that God desires to see come to know Christ. "The Lord is not slow about His promise, as some count slowness, but is patient toward you, not wishing for any to perish but for all to come to repentance." (2 Peter 3:9). Sometimes you remind me of the first apostles, who experienced Pentecost, and preached like Peter. "So then, those who had received his word were baptized; and that day there were added about three thousand souls" (Acts 2:41). It wouldn't surprise me at all, if when you go home, that the Lord will greet you with three thousand souls that were added simply because you shared the Gospel. And though, you may not think it that many, just remember all your **teaching others to teach** the Gospel message.

Trudy, I could go on and on about how you've impacted peoples lives, but this is about how you've impacted my life. You've inspired me with your vision for the Shepherd's Mark, with your prolific witnessing, and also the many, many discussions we've shared about the Bible and specific scriptures. One I remember vividly is a feisty discussion we shared about most preachers preaching, "this is my body broken for you." I pointed out that Jesus broke the bread and said, "this is my body." You were adamant that Jesus didn't have any broken bones, but I thought his body was still broken because it wasn't working, like you would say a toy was broken when it wasn't working the way it should. When you're sick, your body is broken. Jesus' body was broken for us when He hung on the cross. We didn't always agree in our discussions, but they were always a delight to me nevertheless, because you were always so passionate when discussing God's Word. The reality is though, at least for me, that I am overwhelmed by having to summarize such a deep personal friendship over these many years into just a few pages. Just like life, though, "if they were written in detail, I suppose that even the

3

I THOUGHT JESUS WAS A SWEAR WORD

world itself would not contain the books that would be written" (John 21:25). But I have many wonderful memories of phone conversations and visits that are a testimony of your inspiration in my life.

One thing that never ceases to amaze me is your youthful vitality and energy for life. I know that this past year, with the limitations you've faced because of your health, has been extremely difficult for you since you are used to going, and going, and going . . . like the energizer bunny. You, my friend, have been extremely blessed to live such a long and vital life. And even now, you are much more youthful in your vitality than most people your age. There is no doubt in my mind that you will not only see your book published, but if it becomes a best seller the way they are predicting, it will propel the sales of the Shepherd's Mark and you will see your vision finally come to fruition in these last days. "Those who have insight will shine brightly like the brightness of the expanse of heaven, and those who lead the many to righteousness, like the stars forever and ever" (Daniel 12:3). I look forward to celebrating that day with you, and only wish I could have been ~~here to~~ celebrate your 90th birthday too. Enjoy your day!

Infinite Love,

Ann-Marie

4

TRUDY SHERRY AND CAROLYN LAWSON

I have only met Trudy once. She and Carolyn came to stay with in October (2018) during the Fall Festival. I never let people come to stay during that time because I am totally focused on the event and not able to be a good hostess. Carolyn really wanted Trudy to come, so I said yes. I am so very glad I did. Trudy was an absolute delight. Her careful consideration and wise insights amazed me. She was a prayer warrior in advance of the event and enjoyed the many volunteers that circulated about. She had stories to share about events she had coordinated in the past and encouragement for the process as she watched me in a role she knew well. Together we rejoiced over the 33 souls that were changed for eternity as the Gospel was presented.

One of the things we shared during her brief stay was the Shepherd's Mark. It was very interesting to me that she waited until we had time together and got to know each other before she trusted me with her story and creation. She spent time in my home and appeared to be a fruit inspector who wanted to be sure she could share her concept with a kindred spirit. As a dreamer and visionary myself, it was such a blessing to be entrusted with Trudy's treasure. She gifted me with a Shepherd's Mark necklace and shared the way God had

given it to her. I was in awe of the way God worked for years in the life of a saint to prep her for the design He would place in her care.

Trudy's life is a testimony to God's redemptive power design process. As our Creator, who fashioned us in His image, He has made us creators as well. The Shepherd's Mark is the product of a Creator working through a creator to share an eternal message in a tangible way.

Thank you, God, for sharing your creativity and creative process through a seasoned servant. Thank you, Trudy, for being a willing vessel. Well done, good and faithful servant!

Joyce Guthrie
Joshua's Hands

How God opened up a door (literally) to miss Trudy

At 28 years old I never expected to be cleaning houses. I don't say that in a degrading way whatsoever. Just that this isn't the route I ever expected Jesus to take me. But I am so glad He always knows better than we do.

One day I sent a routine text to a new client, or at least I thought. Her name was Carolyn and we had just given her an estimate and sent out a confirmation text of the date and time. Only to receive a very confusing text back not knowing what on earth we were talking about. After a very confusing conversation for both of us I finally realized I had messaged the wrong Carolyn but still couldn't figure out who this mystery Carolyn was and how we had each other's numbers. And as luck, or rather Jesus, would have it, it turned out that this mystery Carolyn was also looking for a house cleaner and asked us over to give her an estimate.

I was sure that upon seeing her I would immediately know who she was. But it wasn't until we began to talk and get to know each other that we realized a mutual friend had introduced us months ago at church because of our shared hearts for human trafficking. I remember her saying, "Oh, I prayed the Lord would send me someone I could trust for this and to be here with my Little Momma!" And I didn't know it then but miss Carolyn and her little momma would end up blessing us more than they could ever know.

Days cleaning at miss Carolyn's quickly became our favorite. Because each day we got to know more and more about little momma. We'd find ourselves spending more time than anticipated just so we could sit and listen to her stories and we wanted to soak up all she had to say.

It wasn't long until we discovered a mutual love for reading and favorite authors. My day would be made at how she would light up over a new book and recall favorite stories, especially stories by Karen Kingsbury. She found so much joy in the little things.

TRUDY SHERRY AND CAROLYN LAWSON

But it wasn't just her love for these books that caught my attention. It was her love for what the books were all about; Jesus. Anytime she spoke you'd feel the presence of the Holy Spirit all over the room. This was a lady who had fought the good fight and had helped countless others do the same. She inspired me more than she could possibly know.

One of my favorite things she would say in the middle of our conversations was, "when God opens a door you better run through it." I'm sure she ran through many doors he opened just for her so she could help to lead others through theirs. A beacon of light for His kingdom.

It's hard to sum up the admiration and love I found for miss Trudy in such a short period of time. I was drawn into her instantly. Her presence, her wisdom, her bluntness that would make us laugh and love her even more. She's one of those rare, one of a kind souls that you never forget.

I will always hold every moment we spent with her dear to my heart. And I pray we get many more of those moments. More of her stories. More of her wisdom and encouragement. I pray she lives to see her book published and that I own one of the first signed copies. A book I'll treasure for the rest of my life.

I never thought I'd be cleaning houses at 28 years old. But praise the Lord I am. And praise the Lord for miss Carolyn's and miss Trudy's. I love you both dearly. We are fervently praying for you and for little momma.

I THOUGHT JESUS WAS A SWEAR WORD

Oh Sweet Miss Trudy! Happy almost 90th Birthday!!! What a blessing it as been to be able to get to know you over the past couple of months. It's been pleasure to say the least. I always look forward to seeing your smiling self every ne we come and clean. The stories you tell us make me smile, and just how assionate you are about everything, fills my heart with JOY! I can just see a idiant light shine in and thru you, and that's the Lord! You are one special lady, iss Trudy! I can't believe you are almost 90!!! I love you!
    Love, Meagan

Church gal
Cleaning gal
In their 20th

Sandy Lassen

Subject: Guess Who's Turning 90?

TO SPECIAL MEMORIES

One, very normal Sunday morning as I sat alone in church a lady sat down next to me. She immediately be-friended me, I was even a little taken back. She had such a genuine sweet smile and I felt instantly drawn to her. I knew she was going to be someone special in my life, and indeed she is. Thank you Jesus. I have so many precious sweet memories of our friendship that it is hard to narrow it down. Trudy, you have helped me to grow in my faith in a very special way. You helped me to realize that Jesus was so much more than my Savior. I learned how real His spirit is that lives within me and the power I have through a simple prayer. We all missed you Trudy, when you left us to move back to Johnson City, but somehow you never really left me. I treasure our telephone calls with you, they always leave me on a high that only special people can do. It's a special gift God has given you. You tell a story with such humor no matter how serious the subject, you always make me laugh and leave me with a smile on my face that just won't go away. My favorite memory is your unique humor about life and about your walk with Jesus. The name of your book "I Thought Jesus was a Swear Word" is the perfect example. It's so you!

To my dear sweet friend, thank you. You will forever be my friend.

I THOUGHT JESUS WAS A SWEAR WORD

> My favorite memory with GG is the extraordinary hug I received from her on Navarre beach. I've only ever experienced that type of hug two other times... from my mamma and daddy. The hug from GG that day felt like home, it felt like all was right in the world, it felt safe. It felt like my savior hugged me through GG.
>
> I love you GG!!
>
> Shannon

> Dear Mom —
> When asked to put together a special memory that we could share with you we decided to combine our efforts as we both chose memories with similar themes. Mom some of my most cherished memories are of my childhood especially our time in the Keys. I have the fond memory of being the conductor of the pelicans. There are so many great memories of that special time and special place and spending it together as a family. Truly one of my favorite things to do when you and Hub came to town to visit would be to take you down to the coast. I loved when you saw our Old Florida it reminded you of the Keys and the special times you all shared as a family. We have always shared a love of the beach. Having you be able to come down to St. George Island for my 50th birthday was very special for Don and I. When we watch sunsets at the coast we will be sure to keep you in our thoughts and hearts.

GG,

I couldn't pick only one memory that was my favorite, so I am going to write about my top four. For starters, one of the best times I've ever spent with you is when I was young and me and KK would come to your house and visit. Now there is no specific moment that makes this one of my favorites, but all of the times spent there with you makes it so special. Another is when you used to teach me and JC about Christianity at our kitchen table. We would sit there for hours with you while you told us your stories and taught us many things we never knew. Some more recent memories are when you had to go to the doctor and I went with you. It was just the spending time with you while you were doing your day to day activities that made me enjoy this day. My last memory that I will mention is one where you and I were in Grammie's living room and I was showing you new music and we were just hanging out and having a good time. I love you. Thank you for providing me with many wonderful memories.

— Bella ♥ xoxo

★

My favorite memory with you GG will always and forever be your famous hugs. Whenever I'm in your arms I know that everything will be okay. Hope you feel the same. I love and miss you more than you know.

lots of love, Gia ♥

I THOUGHT JESUS WAS A SWEAR WORD

Dear GG,

Happy 90th Birthday! I'm so grateful for everything that you have taught me throughout my life. From an early age, you have encouraged me to do good things in this world and to prosper in my faith. If it had not been for you and what you have taught me, I would not be the person, or the Christian that I am today. One of my earlier memories of you is when I was about six and Bella and I were staying the night at your house in Highlands. You took us down to the pond by the house and we watched Triscuit swim. I remember experiencing so much happiness and love whenever we were at your house, but that feeling extends far beyond that house. Those feelings of love and joy follow you around and spread with everything that you do. I hope that you have one of the best birthdays that you have ever had, because you truly deserve it. I love you so much GG!

Love,
Caitlyn ♥

Dear GG,

My favorite memory with you is when we would sit on the couch and you would teach me about Jesus. Another good memory is when I would play my college football game and you would watch me play every night.

Love, JC

TRUDY SHERRY AND CAROLYN LAWSON

11/04/19

My favorite memory with you is when we were all in obx and you me and gabby were all hanging out in the room eating chips and salsa and I was helping you learn to use your first ever smart phone. You got the hang of it quick. Another favorite memory I love is all the times we have talked on the phone. You may be far away but you still kept a smile on my face when talking on the phone. I love you so much GG!

Love Kam♡

My favorite Memory of GG is when she would come into the Kitchen with her child like innocense and take notes on whatever meal I was cooking. Then she would smile so big when she ate whatever we cooked. People in Heaven are going to be happy when GG shows up with her apron on and cooks some great food from all the notes she has taken.

Love,
Ray

I THOUGHT JESUS WAS A SWEAR WORD

My Dearest Aunt Trudy,

This is a little birthday note to tell you how special you are to me and how proud I am to be your niece!

I know I've told you this before, but the fact that you directly impacted myself and my mom and dad for eternity can never be overstated! I remember as a kid thinking you guys in Florida were kinda "different" you know, and that we were the "normies"!... Little did I know!! OK, fast forward a little to 1975 when the Holy Spirit opened my eyes to my need for Jesus Christ - I mean, turned me around on a dime in my thinking.. and I know now that it was a direct answer to your prayers for our salvation.

Oh my goodness Aunt Trudy ... what can I say?? How great a gift to a life is that!!! God rewards the faithful. I remember a pastor saying this: "God puts a special premium on faithfulness" and I believe that to be true. Daniel 12:3 makes me think of you.. "and they that be wise shall shine like the brightness of the firmament; and they that turn many to righteousness like the stars forever and ever. That's how I think of you .. shining for Jesus .. telling others about Him and living the life to back it up.

29

I remember a number of years ago you telling me about how the Holy Spirit leads you and about all the miraculous works of God you were experiencing and seeing in the lives of others. I thought... I don't see that going on here??!! (Of course this is Los Angeles... but seriously!)... here I've been to Bible college, have had the best most gifted bible teaching in and outside the churches I've attended etc., but I am definitely missing out on what I think is supposed to be the normal Christian life — that abiding in Christ adventure - that keeping in step with the Spirit... what you have been living all these years! ☺ I have come to realize that you have shown me it is the faith of a child. Taking God at His Word and just doing it that is the difference between being religious and knowing God. I'm so thankful for your genuine faith albeit across the miles - still clearly seen... for of such is the Kingdom of God.

I THOUGHT JESUS WAS A SWEAR WORD

Rod was just saying that often in the Sunday morning prayer group, he and Mom will pray for you with all kinds of adjectives to let the peeps know just how wonderful and Spirit filled you are :) ! He said you are such an encouragement to him!

You are truly one of a kind in every way! There is just no one like you and how blessed is our family because YOU are in it! Uncle Hub was one lucky dude.. I do say that cheekily and with the utmost love & respect for him ♥♥

Aunt Trudy, I love you with all my heart and I just wanted to express some of how I think of you.

xxxxx Love, Robin ♥♥♥

Chapter 10

A Deathbed Decision

"And a certain man was there, which had an infirmity thirty and eight years. When Jesus saw him lying there, and knew that he had been now a long time in that case, He said unto him, 'Will you be made whole'" (John 5:5–6)?

"And He sent them to preach the kingdom of God, and to heal the sick" (Luke 9:2).

Three months had passed since my last visit to Kendall Children's Home. One day in March, I received a telephone call that my mother was terribly ill. "She's in the hospital, Trudy. She has congestive heart failure, liver infection, a double hernia, emphysema, high blood pressure, kidney breakdown, plus pneumonia."

For a whole month, I asked, "God, how do I pray for this woman? When I was out at Kendall, I would ask you how to pray, and you would show me by your word of knowledge. But, God, this time I don't know what to pray. I can't pray that she will die, and I can't pray she will live and suffer! I just don't know how! What is your will?"

At the end of the month, I received another phone call from my grandmother who was ninety-six years old at the time. "Trudy, get up here to New Jersey right away. Your mother is very, very sick. We don't expect her to live!"

As I hung up the phone, my heart was heavy. I still didn't know how to pray for my own mother!

The next morning, I flew to New Jersey, rented a car at the airport, and drove to Grandmother's house. As I was walking up the sidewalk to the door, Grandmother met me and without even saying hello, she said, "Trudy, go right to the hospital."

I got back into the car and started toward Jersey City. I knew Mother was in a Catholic hospital there, but exactly where it was located was another story! This was at a time before GPS was available. So, calling upon the Lord, I said, "Jesus, show me the way." He did!

As I continued on the right road, a peace came over me. If I happened to turn onto a road going in the wrong direction, this previous peace would leave me and I'd become restless until I got back on the right road again. During this drive to the hospital, I had a tape of Corrie ten Boom called *Faith* playing. It was encouraging to listen to and practice the principles she set before me.

Finally, I came to a place where the road forked. It seemed as if there were two cities in front of me. I was confused as to which road to take because all these towns had their borderlines back to back. On a single pole, there would be *You are now leaving* and *You are now entering* signs. I pulled into a nearby gas station, rolled the window down, and called to the attendant, "Could you tell me where Jersey City is?"

He answered in a curt *Jersey accent,* "You're in it!"

"I'm looking for St. Francis Hospital. Can you tell me where it is?"

He looked at me in a peculiar way then said, "You crazy, lady?"

I said, "No, I need to get to the hospital."

Again, he looked at me and answered, "Well, it's right there!"

Following the directions where he pointed, I spotted the building a block down the road to the left. Delighted, I continued on my way, saying, "Thank you, Jesus."

Once inside the hospital, I took the elevator to the fourth floor. All the way up to my mother's room, I was saying, "Lord, it's been three years since I've seen Mom. Lord, give me the peace that passes all understanding. I don't know what is waiting for me. Lord, I don't want my witness for you to be shaken."

I walked into the doorway of her room and froze. No amount of preparation or prior knowledge of her condition could have prepared me for what I faced. Here my mother lay—once a strong woman, a former schoolteacher. She had also worked for the county clerk at the courthouse helping lawyers. She had changed so that I was stunned. Her once brown hair had become grey and physically she was a mess. Oxygen was going, and all sorts of needles were stuck in her arms with tubes and bottles attached. Because of being an alcoholic, she had also retained thirty pounds of fluid. She was so swollen I could hardly recognize her! The tears came as I prayed, "God, tell me! How do I pray for her? What do I say to her? I'm scared! I need you to tell me! Why aren't you telling me? What's wrong?"

Then, suddenly, the peace and calm I needed came. God had heard me. The aide who had been feeding Mother left the room, and I moved to stand at the foot of the bed. Mother kept staring at me with eyes that bulged. She knew she was dying, and the fear of it showed in those eyes that were so oversized! Slowly, I walked around to the side of her bed. She continued to stare at me, and then must have realized who I was. She grabbed my hand and squeezed it really hard. I sat with her for about thirty minutes without saying anything, letting her adjust to the fact I was there.

Finally, I said, "Mom, can you hear me?" She nodded.

I had to be honest with her, so I said, "Mom, I don't know how to pray for you, but I've asked God to show me. You know I believe that Jesus Christ heals. I know you know that Donald was healed. Do you remember?"

She answered, "Yes."

I knew Mother was familiar with the Bible because she had minored in religion at Adelphi College. I looked at her, and it was at that moment that the Holy Spirit gave me knowledge of what to say.

"Mom, do you remember the story where Jesus talked to the man at the pool of Bethesda? The man had been sick for thirty-eight years, a cripple. Jesus looked at him as if to say, 'Do you really want to be healed?' In other words, every time that man was to get in the pool to be healed, he gave reasons or excuses why he never quite made it."

Then I said, "Mom, I just have to ask you that question before I can even pray for you! Do you really want to be healed? I know I can pray and you will be healed. I have that kind of faith. But I have to know if you really want this!"

She lay still for a while and then said, "Yes."

All I could think of now was "Oh, my goodness, now what do I do? I don't even know if she's a Christian or not!"

I had shared with Mother three years before but still didn't know where she stood with the Lord. Then a new thought wandered through my head. "I know in the Bible they laid hands on people. No, Lord, I can't do that!"

He answered, "Trudy, why are you so worried about what others think? Why don't you do what I say?"

So I took my hand and began to play with a lock of hair on her forehead. How silly and foolish I felt. I thought, *I'm still worried about what these people think. Lord, forgive me.*

Gently but firmly, I placed my hand on her head and said, "Father, I pray that you heal this beautiful woman in body, soul, and spirit. I pray this in the name of Jesus Christ for your glory."

Mother fell asleep then. Peace seemed to flood her face, and her eyes that had been so strained and oversized relaxed.

I sat with her as she slept peacefully for three hours. While I prayed and talked with Mom, I had been aware of others in the room. Now I took time to survey who was there. Mother was just one of six other women in the ward. I noticed that all of them had rosary beads in their hands. But I was very much aware of them watching me praying for Mother. That's what made it so difficult. Now they continued to watch me.

After sitting for those hours, my younger sister came in. We just looked at each other for a moment, then our emotions took over for a time. It had been two years since I had seen Fran.

Seven years earlier, she and her husband had become Christians while they were visiting us in Miami.

But Fran was there now and talking to me. "Trudy, I'm so glad you were here first. I prayed all the way here that you would be. I don't know how to handle this."

Oh, we made a fine pair. She, not knowing how to handle the situation, and me, not knowing how to pray for Mom! Now Fran is a nurse. She is in charge of the supervisors of many nursing home hospitals. She knows her business. So when she asked me if I knew how serious it all was, all I could answer was "Yes."

"Fran," I added. "You know I prayed for Mom that she would be healed. She fell asleep and has been sleeping for at least three hours."

She replied, "Trudy, I think we had better sit down and pray together."

The other five women in that room weren't missing much, but Fran and I clasped our hands and began praying. Just as we began, though, Mother woke and looked over where we were sitting. Recognizing Fran, she asked, "What are you doing?"

Fran turned to me to say, "You sit there and pray." She was pointing to a chair near the foot of the bed. "I'm going to find out where she stands with Jesus."

My only thought was, *I don't know how to pray, and she says pray!* I said aloud, "Fran, I don't know how to pray for Mom anymore."

That answer didn't faze Fran, for she just replied, "Trudy, then pray for me while I talk to her."

Turning toward the bed again, Fran said, "Mother, can you hear me?" Mom nodded.

"Mom, we all want to go to heaven some day with all of us as a family together. Now I could leave here tonight and while driving to Grandmother's house, I could be killed. Mom, I know I'll be going to heaven. I'm a Christian. I know that everyone in my family is a Christian. So is Trudy's whole family. Mom, we're just not sure if you are. In John 14:6, Jesus says, 'I am the way, the truth and the life. No one comes to the Father but through me.' Mom, we don't know if you know Jesus! I've got to know because when we get to heaven, I want to be sure you'll be there, too."

Peace again flooded over her face, and she literally glowed!

"Jesus?" she said. "Yes, I know about Jesus. When I was sixteen, I ran into trouble. I searched and searched and met Jesus. Guess I walked away from what happened."

The tears flooded from Fran's eyes. I, too, felt tears, as I thought of how it had been three years since we prayed for her. As the tears came, I thanked Jesus for such a blessing. I remembered He had healed my son, my eyes, and had led all in my family to himself. Amidst the tears, I again thanked and praised God. But as I continued in this deep-hearted attitude of gratefulness, I realized I was speaking in a language unknown to me. I had never experienced it before, but I found it delightful. The sound of it matched my thanksgiving mood perfectly.

In the meantime, Fran turned to me, tears of joy coursing down her face, and asked, "Trudy, did you hear what Mom said?"

"Yes, I sure did! Fran, did you hear what just happened to me? I think I was just now speaking in what the Bible calls *speaking in tongues*."

"Trudy, don't start that stuff!" Her sharp remark stung.

I kept quiet, saying no more. I had no idea what she was so upset about.

We left the hospital shortly after that, and when I arrived at Grandmother's house, I went straight up to take a bath. (Where else can you be assured of complete privacy?) When I turned the water on, I tried again to speak with this new language. I wanted to see if it was real. It was! Peace and joy flooded my spirit and soul. "Lord, is this part of showing me how to pray for others when I don't know the need or your will?" I couldn't wait to get to the scriptures to study what the Word had to say about this *praying in the Spirit!*

The following day was Wednesday. We went to the hospital and found Mother sleeping. We sat down to wait. Fran began looking at the other five women around the room. She had a tremendous burden for them all.

She said to me, "Trudy, sit there and pray, while I share with some of these women. Do you have your Bible?"

I handed it to her, as she went over to one of the women who was in a great deal of pain. This woman was waiting for the third operation on a slipped disc. Fran shared the scriptures concerning Jesus's love, forgiveness, healing, and eternal life. This lady on the spot asked Jesus into her heart, then proceeded to get out of bed—all pain gone—and walked into the next room to share Jesus with someone over there. That lady, too, asked Jesus into her life. Fran went to each woman in Mother's room.

Just as we were returning to sit with Mother, a Puerto Rican lady waved her fingers, signaling for me to come over to her. This was a little Pentecostal lady with ten children. She said to me, "I want you to know that I know you are Christians. I have been praying for your mother, and I'm praying for all of you."

The lady directly opposite Mom was from Poland, and the lady with whom she had shared in the other room was Cuban. This Cuban woman told us later, "My little baby, my little baby. She two years old. Out on ledge five floor up. I pray, asking Jesus come to me. My baby turn around and fall back into room, not down to street." After accepting Christ, she went home and came back to visit her friend and told us this story.

The lady next to Mom was Italian. The lady next to this lady was Puerto Rican. She spoke very little English, but the Cuban lady from the other room came to share Jesus with this lady.

These women were all from different cultures. In fact, there was one woman from Czechoslovakia who had become ill and had escaped from that country. She couldn't speak English, but she would hold up her rosary and smile.

Later, at Grandmother's house, Fran and I shared with Grandmother. She, too, now knew Jesus. The lady who took care of Grandmother wanted Jesus, too, after asking Fran and I what it was that made us so joyful in the midst of tragedy. What rejoicing! "Lord Jesus, thank you!"

Fran and I returned to the hospital the next day, Thursday. As we sat again with Mom, we shared what the Lord had been doing. Fran said this reminded her of her time in Vietnam.

Barbara, our eldest sister, arrived. She was a picture of despair. She was overcome by her emotions. She wasn't a Christian at the time, so I gave her Corrie ten Boom's tape on *Faith* to listen to at the hospital.

Back at Grandmother's house later that night, we received word that Mother's condition had become critical.

"Her congestive heart failure has worsened, her kidneys have begun to slow down, and she is comatose. You had better get her affairs in order."

I hung up the phone. But even with this grim news, Fran and I remained in a state of joy and peace. We both knew we were completely in God's will and that He had the situation in his control.

That Friday morning, we got the banking business taken care of. We made funeral arrangements, and then returned to the hospital to await Mom's certain death. When we saw her, she was blue, from her hands to her elbows. She was having an awful time breathing even in an oxygen tent! As we waited, Fran continued to share with each new patient who was assigned to the room. As she talked with each one, I enjoyed praying in the Spirit to myself for each person's need.

Saturday, no change took place in Mother. But later that night, after Fran and I had gone to bed at Grandmother's house, Barbara came into our room, saying, "I don't know this Jesus you've got. I need answers for my marriage and for my children." She began to cry, and Fran shared how she could know Jesus.

What rejoicing! Satan's hold on our home and family had been broken. What a joyous sleep we had that night.

Around five o'clock in the morning, the Holy Spirit woke Fran. He put Psalm 107:10–35 on her mind. She woke me, saying, "Trudy, listen to this!

"They dwelt in darkness and gloom, bondsmen in want and in chains, because they had rebelled against the words of God and scorned the counsel of the Most High. And He humbled their heart with trouble; when they stumbled, there was no one to stop them. They cried to the Lord in their distress; from their troubles He rescued them. And He led them forth from darkness and gloom and broke their bonds asunder. Let them give thanks to the Lord for His kindness and His wondrous deeds to the children of men, because He shattered the gates of brass and burst the bars of iron.

"Stricken because of their wicked ways and afflicted because of their sins, they loathed all manner of food, so that they were near the gates of death. They cried to the Lord in their distress; from their straits He rescued them. He sent forth His word to heal them and to snatch them from destruction. Let them give thanks to the Lord for His kindness and His wondrous deeds to the children of man. Let them make thank offerings and declare His works with shouts of joy.

"They who sailed the sea in ships, trading on the deep waters, these saw the works of the Lord and His wonders in the abyss. His command raised up a storm wind which tossed its waves on high. They mounted up to heaven; they sank to the depths; their hearts melted away in their plight. They reeled and staggered like drunken men, and all their skill was swallowed up. They cried to the Lord in their distress; from their straits He rescued them. He hushed the storm to a gentle breeze, and the billows of the sea were stilled; they rejoiced that they were calmed; and He brought them to their desired haven. Let them give thanks to the Lord for His kindness and His wondrous deeds to the children of men. Let them extol Him in the assembly of the people and praise Him in the council of the elders.

"He changed rivers into desert, water springs into thirsty ground, fruitful land into salt marsh, because of the wickedness of its inhabitants. He changed the desert into pools of water, waterless land into water springs."

"Trudy, do you think God is speaking to us? Do you think Mother has been healed? Oh, let's find a church where they preach about Jesus and go this morning." Barbara went with us.

The church we went to was huge. It was a gorgeous building, completely packed with 2,000 people. There was a Bible college connected with it; so many, many young people attended.

Toward the end of the minister's sermon, he asked those who had recently asked Jesus into their lives to raise their hands. Barbara raised hers. The minister then asked for those to come up front to stand up for Jesus. Barbara then declared to us, "Not me. I'm scared."

Since Fran sat on one side of Barbara and I on the other, we both stood up, helping Barbara up with us. We went forward, the three of us, and stood at the altar. Barbara professed publicly her acceptance of Jesus. Each of us did, except we did it as three sisters together!

The pastor then prayed, "Because you have stood up here, Jesus will now stand up before the Father for you."

Leaving church, we stopped for lunch at a nearby restaurant. It was a little after twelve noon when we arrived. We talked until about 2:00 p.m. when we returned to the hospital.

As we stepped off the elevator at the fourth floor, we were in the middle of confusion. Women were standing in the doorways of their rooms, excitedly urging us, "Hurry!" We reached the door of Mother's room and froze! Sitting up in the oxygen tent was Mom, very much alive and well!

She called to us, "Well, where have you girls been?"

Mom really did want to be healed! And she was! I asked the other women in the room when all this had taken place, and they told me it happened a little before noon—the very time Barbara, Fran, and I—Mom's three daughters—stood publicly, saying in effect, we belong to Jesus.

*****

A year later, I was talking with Mom. I persisted in finding out for sure if she knew Jesus personally. I still had no peace about it. I knew that she had heard about Jesus, knew all about Him, and believed on His name. But I needed to find out if she had ever asked Him personally into her life. I needed to know if she had the assurance that God had forgiven her sins. I wanted to be sure she knew He could be depended upon to take control of her life in order to make her the kind of person He wanted her to be.

The assurance came, and I shared with her what had taken place at the hospital those days she was so ill.

"Mom, all during that week you were in the hospital, all those women in your room became Christians. So did others who came in and out of your room, including aides, patients, and nurses."

Tears were falling, as she said, "It was just like in the book of Acts! It's like Jesus is walking on Earth again! I thank God for you, girls, praying for.me."

Everyone in our family had become Christians and many of the broken relationships have been healed. Why? Because each of us truly *really wanted to be healed.*

Chapter 11

Miami Prayer Rally with Corrie Ten Boom

"If my people, which are called by my name, shall humble themselves, and pray; and seek my face, and turn from their wicked ways, then will I hear from heaven, and will forgive their sin, and will heal their land" (2 Chronicles 7:14).

I had a burden for women, but all I kept getting from God was 2 Chronicles 7:14. I couldn't understand what He was saying. I had the opportunity to go to Dallas, Texas. Campus Crusade for Christ is now known as Cru. They hosted an event called Explo '72. There were 100,000 people in attendance! We were at a seminar on how to conduct Bible studies, and I was restless. Suddenly, a friend grabbed me by the arm and began dragging me to another meeting. "I don't want to go!" I protested. But I did. I found myself in a lecture (entitled *The Great Commission Prayer Crusade*) conducted by Vonette Bright, wife of Campus Crusade's President, Bill Bright. After her talk, I told her that I was the prayer chairman of a large Christian school that my children attended. I asked her if this could be done on a smaller scale with the mothers. "I don't see why not" was her reply.

So I returned to Miami with the burden of setting up prayer groups among mothers in schools. We establish them according to grade levels so we could pray for some urgent concerns. There were many needs—complacency in the school, discipline problems, drugs, and occult influence which was moving in.

At the next monthly women's meeting, there was 200 in attendance. I boldly told them I felt the Holy Spirit was leading us to form prayer groups in the school. I had experienced the power of prayer in my own life. I extended an invitation to anyone that was interested. I was scared to death when forty-eight women signed up. It hit me that it was an awesome responsibility I had accepted. What was the Holy Spirit leading us into?

At that point, whenever I started praying, I would see the city of Miami with prayer groups all over the city. This vision was coupled with 2 Chronicles 7:14 and what I had heard at the Campus Crusade meeting about their setting up citywide neighborhood prayer groups. The plan, starting with a prayer rally in the city, would bring all the Christians together in prayer for unity in the home, city, and nation. If this was to take place in Miami, I knew the keynote speaker had to be very special. We had Jewish and Cuban communities expanding, plus the occult influence growing. There was no real unity in the body of Christ in Miami. What we did have was extreme complacency. How could all this come about?

My husband had a convention to attend in San Francisco. He invited me to join him. We left a week early to attend an *Institute in Basic Youth Conflicts* led by Bill Gothard in Long Beach, California. The Home for CC (Campus Crusade) for Christ was located near San Francisco. Specifically, it was in San Bernardino at the time. As the week progressed, I couldn't shake the recurring idea to go and visit Vonette Bright. I continued to feel God's strong direction to proceed. I went and shared with Vonette's secretary what was happening in Miami. In order for us to put on a prayer rally, we would need an outstanding speaker. We asked for her insight, but she suggested several names. Not one clicked in my spirit until she mentioned one who was speaking at a rally in Long Beach that week. Her name was Corrie ten Boom. Of course, perfect! I had read all of her books and heard most of her tapes and was familiar with her love and sacrifices for Jewish people. Miami Beach, being predominately Jewish, would be open to her sharing with them. She was known for her family hiding Jewish people in Holland during WWII.

Saturday morning, I got up and got my two sons and husband off for a fishing trip for the day. I sat in the living room in a chair, unable to do anything but wait for God to move. My daughter was cleaning the house. In the middle of the morning, the doorbell rang. When she answered, her mouth dropped open to see the principal standing there with the tapes in his hands. Cassette tapes were used before CD's.

She turned to me and said, "You really do believe in prayer, don't you?" She them invited him in. He sat on a stool in front of my chair and apologized for keeping the tapes so long. There had been a tremendous response from the teachers after hearing them and they felt the tapes would be a help to many of the parents, especially as the greatest problem among women seemed to be depression. I agreed with him, still not letting him know that this was my condition at that very moment. When he left, Carolyn turned to me and said, "God hears you, and He answers."

I listened to the tapes which helped me stop focusing on myself. I was propelled into action. First, I went to my church and asked them to come and pray with me; they seemed disinterested. Lacking was the understanding or compassion for the mothers of these troubled homes God had showed me. "I'm sure glad I don't live in that" was the reaction. They didn't realize that this was taking place all over the city, in their own neighborhoods, and throughout the nation. Getting no response, I went home with mixed emotions. I was hurting, and I cried out to God to bring someone to me to pray with.

He was faithful, as always. By the end of the week, I received a telephone call from a young man from Atlanta. He had been invited to share his testimony in West Palm Beach in some neighborhood Bible study groups. He had gotten our names from someone in the ATL Campus Crusade who had worked with us. They felt he would enjoy meeting us. We met with Him and Hub shared an offer. We extended an invitation to come home with us. He changed his travel plans, arranging for a morning flight out of Miami International Airport. When we got home, Hub went to bed, since he had to get up early for work. Sitting with me in the living room, this young man looked me straight in the face and said, "My spirit hurts. What is bothering you?" I proceeded to share my concerns with him.

"Trudy, how do you know Jesus like that?" he asked.

I shared my testimony, and when I had finished, he suggested we pray about the situation in the neighborhood. "I don't know how to pray or where to start."

He looked at me and asked, "Do you pray in the Spirit, Trudy?"

I coughed and sputtered because I had told no one that six months earlier I had begun to pray in an unknown language while I was praising God for healing my mother in the hospital.

I knew there was much controversy over praying in the spirit and I didn't want to cause division. But I knew Jesus had given this to me to pray when I don't know how through the Spirit in me.

This man reminded me that the Bible said that when you don't know how to pray in a situation for someone or something you have a burden for, we are instructed to pray in the Spirit. We are to let Him pray through us. Satan can't interpret what you are saying to God, and you aren't trying to tell Him what to do. You are also praying in the perfect will of God, and you aren't trying to tell Him what to do. "Trudy," he advised. "As a Christian, you either have to stay in the neighborhood and let God work through you or move out."

"I've already asked my husband many times to move out of this area, and his response is always the same. These problems are all over the whole US, not just in Miami. Moving would just be an imagined hope of moving away from the problem." I told him that Hub didn't have the same burden as I did and didn't want to become involved. He had helped to organize the homeowners' association to better our neighborhood physically, but in this spiritual situation, he didn't know what to do, either.

"Hmm," he quietly said. "Let's just talk to Jesus, and let the Holy Spirit talk to Jesus through us. Let them decide what they want you to do."

I was scared! Not only had I never told anyone about my praying in the Spirit, I had never heard anyone else pray like this, either. But as he began to pray, I felt like I was in the complete presence of God because there was such a unity in our hearts for Him to hear the burden He had put on my heart. After we finished praying, I knew that God heard. I was just to wait.

Thanksgiving Day passed, and the first of December, I began receiving telephone calls from a woman in my neighborhood who I had met at a Bible study. She was a new Christian. Her daughter had met me through Campus Crusade. She felt burdened to put on a Christmas Coffee for her neighbors. I would speak and share what Christmas meant to me. First, like anyone, I was caught up in the trappings of the holidays. I kept telling her I'd been out of town and I didn't have my Christmas shopping done. Excuses, excuses. I kept turning her down. I saw her again at a Bible study. That night, the Holy Spirit spoke very simply, "Didn't you pray and ask me what you should do and what my will was?" I about choked! That very night, I called her, asking her to forgive me. I went on to tell her that I'd prayed a few weeks before and she was an answer to that prayer. The Christmas Coffee was set for next week.

When I got to her house, she met me at the door, exclaiming, "I had twenty women on my heart to invite and, Trudy, all twenty women have showed up!" She was visibly shaken. I shared how I had learned about Jesus Christ as Lord and Savior and how my family was beginning to be changed. My youngest son had been healed of an incurable disease through prayer. All but one of these women was already Christian and that one accepted Christ that very day. I shared what was happening in our very own neighborhood and we all prayed about it. As women, we joined, united through prayer, to change our neighborhood, city, and country. We knew we were to start specifically in our own homes. We asked God to put them in order as He intended them to be.

The next day, my sixteen-year-old daughter came home from school and asked me if I was the lady that one of her classmates told her about. Her mother had gone to a coffee where a lady shared about the power of prayer and she had never heard anything like it before. That lady also knew Jesus as a personal friend. "Mom, I knew it had to be you! She wants to know Jesus, just like you do," Carolyn glowed.

The Holy Spirit spoke again. "Can you see how this nation can be healed if my people pray together in unity, in one accord for neighborhoods all over this city and nation? I know this is a very hard town because of the spiritual warfare going on, but trust me. I have chosen the Westminster Christian women as the nucleus to start this move in the city."

"But, Lord, where do I start?"

"Take the list of forty-eight names you got at the women's meeting and I will lead the way. I want you to be very sensitive to my voice."

So I sat down with the list and prayed over each name, asking the Lord to give me twelve names to be the head over each grade level. As I looked at the names and prayed over each one, I started to write them down as they seemed to jump out at me. The first one I knew. She held a Bible class for Catholic women, and I knew that she knew Jesus. The second, third, and fourth, I didn't know at all. The others, I knew of. I ended up with seventeen, instead of twelve names, and didn't know what they were for. Later, we discovered they were to help organize and lead teacher prayer groups, coordinate and lead a school board group, and put together a working mothers' night prayer group.

Now I had the names…how was I to proceed? I was reminded of God asking Moses to go to Pharaoh. Moses kept doubting God, until God turned his rod into a snake and then back into a rod again, signifying His power. Just then, the phone rang. I was asked if I'd volunteer my home to be used as the place where people could drop off used clothing for the school bazaar. I decided that the drop-off day would be the day to start telephoning the names on the list. I would be home, anyway, waiting for the clothing.

Since I was the only one who knew that it was God's plan to have a citywide prayer chain, I asked Him to really make it clear that this was really of Him.

The day arrived, and before I could start on my phone, the doorbell rang. I answered it, and the first girl on my list was standing there, holding a new shirt that still had the tags on it. She didn't know why she was there, but she just knew she was to come and bring this one shirt for the bazaar. I was really shaken as I invited her in. I told her what my burden was and what the Spirit had revealed to me. She suggested we pray about it, and after that, she agreed to participate, choosing the grade level she was most comfortable with. After she left, within half of an hour, the doorbell rang again. This girl had a car full of new and used clothing. I didn't know her, and we introduced ourselves. She was the second name on the list! Again, shaken, I invited her in and explained what God had been doing. She was very excited as she had been asking God to be part of *it*—she wasn't sure what *it* was—and had decided to wait on Him and do nothing until He showed her the way. By now, I understand that He was putting it all together. I was able to stay put and let Him do His job.

The next day, the doorbell rang. The third girl on the list was standing there. I knew her. She was as excited as the others. After she left, the telephone rang. "Trudy, I just had to call you. I can't wait any longer and I can't get it out of my mind. I'm calling to tell you I'd like to be one of the leaders to head up a prayer group." When she told me her name, of course, it was the fourth one on my list and I dropped the phone!

Then the Spirit spoke again and said, "Do you need any more proof to show you?" And he gave me Zechariah 4:6, "Not by might, nor by power but by my Spirit, saith the Lord."

With this, I said, "Yes, I believe You, and I will trust You." I then called the remainder of the names, and not one person turned me down.

We had a meeting the following week. We came into a tremendous unity, and within ten days, sixteen prayer groups were established within the school community.

On New Year's Eve, we had our first emergency prayer request. Because all of the chains were interconnected, we were able to send the request through all the chains. The Lord was showing us something very dramatic about the advantages of unity in prayer.

The first request was for Barbara, a recent graduate of Westminster School. Her back was broken, both lungs were collapsed, and a tracheotomy was necessary after she was critically injured in a motorcycle accident. Immediately, all of the prayer groups were activated and countless prayers were offered up to God, upholding Barbara daily, and God honored these prayers. A group of us went to the hospital and prayed with her. In fact, many prayer groups went to the hospital and prayed with her constantly. "Please, Lord, spare her life so that you may be glorified." She was gradually healed of the acute damage but it was her paraplegia that returned her to her faith in Christ.

After New Year's Eve, we realized many people did not know how to pray. God joined me with another woman who shared the mechanics of how to pray conversationally as originated by Rosalind Rinker in a Presbyterian church in New Jersey. I shared the reality of the power of prayer through my personal testimony. The large group to which we were speaking then broke up into small groups where each person actually prayed short, conversational prayers. This first meeting was so successful that we teamed together and started teaching workshops all over Dade County. Twenty-five of them were presented in schools and churches county-wide. We became prayer partners, and I shared with her how I felt this was going to be bigger than just praying for our Christian school. This was to be the nucleus that would start the citywide prayer chain in Miami, originating with the great Commission Prayer Crusade rally sponsored by Cru. Corrie ten Boom would be the speaker.

Having voiced this, I began struggling with how to contact her. At this point in my life, God had raised up a young girl with whom I'd shared and had led to the Lord. She was a long-distance operator, and whenever I prayed about how to find someone or how to contact someone, my telephone number would come up on her board and she would call and ask if she could help me. This happened now, and we decided that we might reach her through Billy Graham. Sure enough, through his people, we discovered she was staying at Cliff Barrow's home. I called there and asked if she would pass this message on to Corrie or her secretary. After much prayer and talk, Corrie had her secretary call me back to say that they had felt the Lord would like her to come to Miami. The only time she would have would be February 26. She would be returning from vacation in the Florida Keys before returning to Holland. I promised I would call back when I located where God wanted the rally to be held.

Calling my prayer partner, I asked her to pray while I was on the phone, calling various auditoriums and convention halls. I had completely forgotten that winter is the time all the *snowbirds* come to Florida. Everything was booked far in advance. I called my prayer partner again and asked if she was praying because all I was getting were nos! She said that she had been receiving a word in her spirit that there would be a cancellation at the Dade County Auditorium. I called them again and asked to talk to the manager. The answer was still no, but because of my persistence—I hadn't given him the date yet—he said, "Who is this Corrie ten Boom?"

I was able to fill him in completely about her life, how she had hidden Jewish people in her home during WWII, and how she and her family had been taken to concentration camps because of their help to the Jewish people. Corrie had been the only family member to survive the camps. When I finished, he said, "Please hold the line a minute."

While waiting, my eye caught his name on a paper in front of me. He was Jewish. When he came back to the line, he said he had one date that he might possibly cancel. "I will cancel it for this Corrie," he stated.

Holding my breath, I asked him what it was. "February 26." The very date (and only date) when she could come! All doubts vanished. God was in control.

TRUDY SHERRY AND CAROLYN LAWSON

For Trudy and Hub, my friends _ _

I THOUGHT JESUS WAS A SWEAR WORD

Message and messenger most welcome in Tampa

THERE IS EXCITEMENT in the air as thousands plan their pilgrimage to Tampa Stadium tomorrow night. And neither the Bucs nor the Rowdies are playing.

The excitement appears to be generated by the people from countless Christian churches in the Tampa Bay area who are convinced that the real message of hope will be delivered here during the next few days by God's famous modern-day messenger, Billy Graham.

Yet the joyous anticipation by the faithful is but a small part of what promises to be a dynamic series of wholesome family occasions specifically designed to provide answers to those who have been vainly searching for meaning in their lives.

The Florida West Coast Billy Graham Crusade has been bathed in prayer, supported by many churches, headed by prominent leaders of our community and state and planned with precision and order. Several thousand counselors have been trained. A massive interdenominational choir of perhaps 5,000 will be rehearsing at the stadium tonight.

It is good that Mr. Graham and his team are among us. We sincerely believe that the people of our community, with a strong Judeo-Christian heritage, are more than ready for a strengthening of their faith — for an emphasis on their spiritual lives, which are so eternal, rather than on their material lives, which are so temporal.

Billy Sunday provided great inspiration for Tampans 60 years ago.

Billy Graham brings his welcome message "home" to Tampa this week.

talented, like Johnny Cash, Norma Zimmer and Myrtle Hall. The crusade, each night through Saturday, and closing Sunday afternoon, will be

TRUDY SHERRY AND CAROLYN LAWSON

Larry
Donna Lynn
Bill Bright
Vonette Bright at recent social gathering
CRU 1973

Miami 'Prayer Chain' Sets National Example

By ADON TAFT
Herald Religion Editor

RELIGION NEWS

A Miami experiment in prayer has become a national model to be described in the February issue of Impact, a magazine published by Campus Crusade for Christ International.

The successful experiment is the Greater Miami Emergency Prayer Chain, organized in its present form last September by Mrs. Hubbard (Trudy) Sherry and now in contact with prayer groups in 30 cities in 19 states and five other countries.

The chain includes the official co-operation of 12 denominations and a network of interdenominational prayer groups in such diverse places as police departments, schools, airlines, the Air Force base, and senior citizen housing projects, to name a few.

The idea, according to Mrs. Sherry, is "to establish a system of communicating to every individual prayer group within Greater Miami the information necessary to achieve the united prayer action of God's people to meet specific, urgent and vital needs of the community, nation and body of Christ."

A LOT of things contributed to the formation of the chain which now has a steering committee of six couples from five denominations, including:

- Presbyterians — Mortgage banker Hub Sherry and his wife, Trudy.
- Episcopalians — School superintendent Dr. Don Burroughs and his wife Noreen.
- Methodists — Lt. Col. Grant Kerber, chief of the Air Rescue Squadron at the Homestead Air Force base, and his wife Myra; and Dr. Neil Frank, head of the National Hurricane Center, and his wife Velma.
- Catholics — Airline pilot Ray Rossman and his wife Mary Ellen.
- Baptists — Developer Roger Heim and his wife Marian.

The first event that laid the groundwork was the Great Commission Prayer Crusade which attracted 2,500 people to Dade County Auditorium some three years ago. It was organized by the Sherrys.

IN THE following two years, more than 200 prayer groups sprang up throughout the city. They met in homes, businesses, schools, hospitals and in churches. The Sherrys tried to keep track of them.

Then in December 1974, Chris Carrier, a 10-year-old boy returning home from school, was kidnaped in Coral Gables. Mrs. Sherry began to link some of those groups together in a bond of prayer for the missing boy.

Chris was beaten, shot and abandoned in the Everglades, but he was found a week later, returned home, and miraculously recovered almost completely.

Many, including Mrs. Sherry and the Carrier family, considered prayer to be the key factor in the sparing of Chris's life. So the concept of the emergency prayer chain began to take form in Trudy's mind.

"IT WAS based on the sure knowledge that God wants and expects His faithful people to intercede, through prayer, for the needs of an individual, a situation, a community, a people, a nation, His world," explained Mrs. Sherry, who referred to the passage of Scripture found in II Chronicles 7:14.

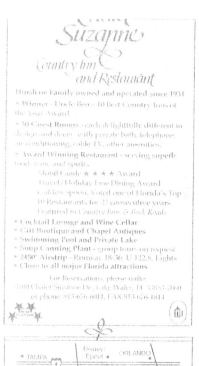

CHAPTER 12

Lord Teach Us to Pray

"If ye abide in me, and my words abide in you, ye shall ask what ye will, and it shall be done unto you" (John 15:7).

God was in control! If I hadn't been assured of that, the mammoth task ahead would have been too much. I called my prayer partner to share what her leading had led to. I pled for her continued prayers for the organizing of the Campus Crusade for Christ rally. I called Corrie's secretary to confirm her availability. Prayer groups joined in unity, asking Jesus to guide and direct each step. Needs were written down and, one by one, they were prayed for.

Then we waited for answers and acted on them as they came. We were given a leadership steering committee composed of seventeen people and a secretary with the ability to implement their spirit-led decisions. The program had to be designed—music, leader, worship groups, a soloist (who knew he had been led to Miami for a definite purpose), a staging coordinator, and a Latin American called to share a testimony and speak for the large Spanish population of the city. Prayers were answered as we had volunteers commit. All of these details came together, orchestrated by the Holy Spirit. But what about finances? We prayed about them.

We needed $6,000 to cover the costs of the rally; this included Spanish-translating equipment and materials for an ongoing work afterward. By the day of the rally, $5,594 had been donated, completely unsolicited. Prayer had brought it in as the Spirit moved. An additional $1,305 was turned in with registration slips the night of the rally, giving a total of $6,899.00. Because of ongoing work in Spanish and Black communities, six months after the rally, $500 more was needed. After two weeks of prayer, it was discovered it had been donated by an anonymous Miami businessman.

Over 2,300 people gathered in the auditorium that night, not only to hear Corrie ten Boom's powerful message but also the testimony of a refugee who arrived in Miami from Chile on the evening of February 25! The Cuban Christians had been praying for the release of this young man who could share his testimony at the rally. As they were praying, God revealed to them to pray for something bigger. What God had in mind was something they didn't know until the night he arrived. Here is the testimony of this young man from Chile and his greater prayer request:

"People in Miami have been praying for me as Communism has been taking over my country. There are many difficulties I encountered in red tape and paperwork. I praise the Lord that I was able to get out. I appreciate the prayers of my friends here in Miami. The people will have the opportunity to vote for or against the Marxist government. Many Chileans are seeking a better government. The request I have for you tonight are your prayers for Chile."

After his talk, we all united together as one body, earnestly seeking God's perfect will in the Chile elections, prayer being led by Corrie ten Boom. We continued praying until we knew the election was over. How we praised God for answering our prayers when the newspapers reported that the Communists in Chile had not gained the election which had been predicted!

The rally resulted in God providing five hundred volunteers to begin the Greater Miami Emergency Prayer Chain. Over two hundred prayer groups were started in the city, and four meetings were held during the year by prayer captains to teach them how to pray.

At the Christian school where the prayer group originated, there were five prayer workshops for mothers that year and sixteen prayer groups were started. The senior high school students began a monthly prayer breakfast. The teachers planned a conversational prayer workshop for themselves and their spouses for March. A newsletter was sent out to all school families.

The churches were touched, too. Seven of them held conversational prayer workshops.

Husband and wife prayer teams were formed, other new prayer groups were started in many churches, and five women were burdened to be used to present prayer workshops and begin groups in nursing homes. A church troubled without a minister sent delegates to a workshop who returned and set up prayer groups in the congregation. "A miracle is happening here!" they exclaimed.

In spite of the many people I prayed with and for constantly, I didn't have any one special prayer partner who I could depend upon for deep spiritual support. I began to ask God to send the right person—one He would choose for me and me for her. Soon after, I went to my usual bowling league game and I was led to talk to a woman I had known casually as a league member for several months. Little did I know that she, too, had been praying about a special concern. Beverly's whole life had been lived in the Christian faith, and yet she could never achieve the close relationship to Jesus Christ that she longed for. She was asking God how to get it. Then I came *out of the blue*. As we talked, I found myself sharing with her my experiences of meeting Jesus as my personal Savior and my recent encounter with the Holy Spirit. From 1973 until Bev's death, we have been united in His spirit and have upheld each other and our families through all the storms of our lives.

My prayer partner and I were invited to Orlando to hold a prayer workshop for Christian leaders who have responded to the need for prayers in their city. Our husbands also were invited to come and tell how their lives and homes have begun to change as a result of these prayer groups. Mrs. Askew, the governor's wife at the time, held a coffee to share the results and impact of the Great Commission of Prayer Ministry. The possibility of it being spread statewide in Florida was discussed.

Countless individual prayers were specifically answered through the year as a result of the citywide prayer groups, such as a man's sight being restored, a woman without time for Christ went through two heart attacks yielded her life to Him and was healed, another's eyesight was restored, a finger was healed, and a leg was saved from amputation.

Being the coordinator for all these prayer groups that emerged, I began receiving calls from the leaders who were floundering for answers to serious situations which had begun to arise within their groups. Neither they nor their pastors could answer them. I began to realize that many, many women did not know how to pray. Many were embarrassed to admit this. As I sought the Lord in prayer, all I could hear in the spirit was "Lord, teach us to pray!" I went to the scriptures and asked what He was trying to tell me. As I studied Luke 11:1–4, the Holy Spirit spoke, "Remember, the disciples were standing with Jesus when they asked Him that, but these leaders are not standing next to Him since He is now with the Father. Rather, Jesus gave us the Holy Spirit to guide us—to teach us."

Teach us! Wow! That is how He led me to compile a prayer booklet, using twenty-five of the finest writing on the practice of prayer. I also shared testimonies of answered prayer in a variety of circumstances. This was the basis for the prayer workshops that we taught. I found these workshops gave the women confidence in how to pray and taught them how to pray in specific areas. They had not seen or experienced how to pray God's word as it applied to certain situations. The women's prayer lives, Bible time, and Bible studies become more personal, alive, and more meaningful after the workshops. He will bless all who fulfill His conditions, and then know they can wait expectantly for His promises to come.

People are crying to God for an answer, sometimes not knowing why they cry. God has heard the cry and has sent His Son, and in turn has sent us to proclaim Him—quietly, daily, without fanfare.

Chapter 13

Kidnapped and Left for Dead

2/20/1997

Dear Chris,

My name is Trudy Sherry. I am writing this letter to you so you can hear (like Paul Harvey says) *the rest of the story*. I have tried to reach you for many years through a variety of ways, but especially through Rick Sloan (an alumni of Westminster Christian School). My children, Carolyn and Don, also went to WCS. Carolyn recently went to her twenty-year reunion and started receiving the alumni mailer. It was there I saw your picture with your mom and brother. In the last six months, I also received a news interview my prayer partner, Beverly Castetter, recorded from a Miami Station. Then I got some phone calls after your interview with Oprah. After MAN magazine carried your story, I started to pursue contacting you so you can know how your life and the tragedy that happened to you really became *what Satan intended for evil, God has turned for good.*

I have taught prayer workshops for twenty-five years. I was the prayer chairman at Westminster Christian School. Originally, I began setting up prayer groups for the moms of each grade level. Next the Lord led me to organize and lead a prayer rally in Miami. It was sponsored by Campus Crusade for Christ. Carrie ten Boom was the key note speaker. Two hundred city and school-wide prayer groups emerged as a result of that effort. We attended Granada Presbyterian Church in Miami. The prayer groups were going strong. It was after a 1973 prayer rally that the Lord gave me a vision of a prayer chain that could break denominational lines and reach into neighborhood schools and cities. He directed me to contact pastor prayer leaders from a variety of denominations as we carved out a new walk in faith.

At this point, in 1974, we left Granada and became a part of an international group in Homestead. This was when I decided to form a small emergency prayer chain. We started with a *small* group of 150 to 200 people. We wanted to try at a local level before we went city or statewide. At the same time, other local churches matched our effort. Little did we know God was preparing us to play such a vital part in your life.

We established prayer group, linking them together with individual prayer partners and guidelines to follow. There were young and older people, men and women—all people who loved Jesus and believed He was capable of dramatically changing lives. We had experienced many tremendous answers to prayer in our own family and we organized and waited expectantly.

The first emergency request to come in was about a little boy who had been abducted. Now you see why I am writing.

I called each lead chain person and conveyed what we knew. I told them to pray but to call me back if God showed them anything in their prayer times. No matter how trivial it seemed they were encouraged to call and report back.

On the third day after you were kidnapped, three girls were praying when the Lord gave one of the girls a picture of you. You were lying on what appeared to be in the everglades, critically injured. They cried out to the Lord on your behalf, asking Him to send angels to protect you and keep you safe until you were found.

Then she saw what looked like Jacob's ladder and angels coming down and surrounding you. They called and reported this. I entered into our prayer log.

The fourth day, another call came. Two guys prayed together. One of them saw a picture of a man in a house. He was able to see the house and surrounding area, but not facial details of the man. He felt he was contemplating suicide. He called and wanted to know if he should call the police. He thought he recognized the house because he had lived in that area. I told him he should go back to prayer and plead for his life and his salvation. We wanted God to get all the glory. The other prayer chain members were contacted and instructed to pray for the man's life and salvation. They were to continue to intercede on your behalf, praising God for His protection of you. I also told the ones wondering about going to the police that wherever there was something of spiritual value, there was always counterfeit. We were not like the psychics, and we didn't want the police to think we were nuts. At that time, there was a lot of resistance to the newly labeled *charismatics*. These were simply young people who had come to Christ and seen Him dramatically change their lives. They were not radicals or into a cult, they just loved Jesus and believed He cared enough about a little boy lying bleeding and left alone to die. They prayed like they had never prayed before, hoping and believing that their prayers would make a difference.

When you were found, we realized that what God showed them was for real. Your story inspired the prayer chains to just take off. What an impact it is when something works!

I started teaching women's prayer workshops. I incorporated your story into inspiring women to discover what happened when they earnestly seek his face, we moved to Clearwater, Florida, and, eventually, I coordinated the prayer ministry for the Billy Graham Crusades (beginning in 1978).

We have since moved to a small town in North Carolina. Ironically, one of the teachers who was at WCS when you were there goes to our church.

I would love to hear from you to put the other pieces of the prayer puzzle together.

Chris, thank you for allowing your story to impact the body of Christ like it has.

In Christ,
Trudy Sherry

The New York Times
ARCHIVES 1996
Forgiven and Befriended By Victim, Attacker Dies
Oct. 6, 1996

About the Archive

This is a digitized version of an article from The Times's print archive, before the start of online publication in 1996. To preserve these articles as they originally appeared, The Times does not alter, edit or update them.

Occasionally the digitization process introduces transcription errors or other problems. Please send reports of such problems to archive_feedback@n5rtimes.com.

Chris Carrier recently went to visit his ailing elderly friend at a nursing home in North Miami Beach. He took along a pound of the friend's favorite fish treat, smoked amberjack, comforted the man and made sure that he was warm and well taken care of.

It was the last time that he saw his friend, who died later that night.

The friend, David McAllister, was a blind, frail and lonely 77-year-old with no one to look after him. He had also recently confessed to abducting, stabbing and shooting Mr. Carrier in the head and leaving him in the Everglades 22 years ago.

The survival of Mr. Carrier, who was 10, stunned Miami in 1974. Last month, he shocked people again by forgiving and befriending the man who had confessed to the crime.

Now Mr. Carrier has been waiting to learn about funeral arrangements, as Mr. McAllister's body remains unclaimed at Columbia Aventura Hospital, where he died on Sept. 26. The cause of death was not released. Mr. McAllister left no names of family members, and Mr. Carrier is about the only person who wants to pay last respects.

"This provided closure for him," Mr. Carrier said. "He wanted to say, 'I'm sorry,' and I wanted to tell him, 'No harm done.'"

Mr. Carrier was blinded in his left eye as a result of the shooting, but he said he did not feel that he had been permanently traumatized, adding that he bore no ill will toward the man who had kidnapped him and left him to die.

"It wasn't hard for me to show compassion, given his circumstances," said Mr. Carrier, who is married, has two daughters and until recently worked as a youth minister. "I moved on. This event did not haunt me all my life."

After Mr. McAllister was questioned last month for the first time in 21 years by the original detective on the case, Maj. Charles Scherer of the Coral Gables police, he confessed to having abducted Mr. Carrier and leaving him on Dec. 20,1974. A fifth grader at Westminster Christian School, Mr. Carrier had gone home early from school on the last Friday before the Christmas vacation. He had left the bus and was walking home along Aledo Avenue in Coral Gables.

Mr. McAllister tricked him into going into his motor home, stabbed him with an ice pick and drove him to a desolate spot, where he shot the boy in the head from behind. An extensive search followed, with a $10,000 reward.

The boy was unconscious for six days. He awoke the day after Christmas and was rescued by a farmer who was driving by. The side of his head was bloody. He had two black eyes, light stab wounds in the chest and cigarette burns.

A bullet had entered at the left temple and exited at the right temple, injuring the optic nerve and closing the eye.

Mr. Carrier speculated that the burns, some of which still scar him, were meant to test whether he was dead.

Mr. Carrier remembered little about those six days. "It was more traumatic for my parents and my brother," he said. "It was a walk in the park for me. It happened so fast."

From the beginning, Mr. McAllister was a prime suspect. He had been dismissed six months before by Mr. Carrier's father, Hugh, from his job taking care of an elderly uncle. Mr. McAllister also had a long criminal record, owned a motor home and bore an uncanny resemblance to a composite sketch made from the boy's recollections. The problem was that there was no physical evidence linking Mr. McAllister to the crime.

But Major Scherer was sure that Mr. McAllister was the assailant. When the police went to question him in 1975, he behaved as though he was expecting the police to find him and charge him with the crime, Major Scherer recalled, adding: "He said to the investigators: 'What took you all so long? I've been expecting you.' Everything was there—the motive, the motor home and the composite picture, almost identical. But we couldn't get Chris to identify him."

Major Scherer received word in August that Mr. McAllister was a patient at the Greynolds Park Manor nursing home and went to interview him.

"He was defensive at first," Major Scherer said. "He eventually confessed to picking up Chris and driving him out there, but not to stabbing or shooting him."

The first time that Mr. Carrier visited Mr. McAllister at the home, after Major Scherer had been in contact with him, he began to cry when he realized that the young man before him was the boy whom he had hurt and abandoned.

"When he was asked what he did," Mr. Carrier said, "he sort of gasped and said, 'I left him there,' and began to cry. He said he was sorry, and I told him I forgave him and that from now on there would be nothing like anger or revenge between us, nothing except a new friendship."

Mr. Carrier visited Mr. McAllister frequently over the next three weeks. They often prayed together and read.

"I'm glad he was able to put the past behind him," Mr. Carrier said. "I tried to let him know he had a friend."

A version of this article appears in print on October 6, 1996, on Page 1001034 of the National edition with the headline: Forgiven and Befriended By Victim, Attacker Dies.

© 2019 The New York Times Company

CHAPTER 14

Lose Him and Let Him Go

Everyone experiences times of darkness and confusion. It is during those times where all hope seems lost that God's voice and His Word will break through and show His faithfulness.

While sitting at my desk, writing out my bills for the month, I wrote on a pad all that I had to do to complete before getting ready to go on an exciting trip to Europe. The next chore on my list was to get our suitcases from the furnace room in the lower level of the house. All of a sudden, a gentle but firm voice of the Holy Spirit spoke dearly to me, "Get your suitcases *now*." It was so instinctive to obey when it is that abrupt and specific and you know that voice you are hearing is His. (My sheep know my voice). I went downstairs, and as I passed the sliding glass doors to the lower porch, I glanced at a disturbance that caught my eye outside the door. Here was a small bird flopping over and over as it seemed to be hurt, and no matter how hard it tried to get free, it just kept flopping over and over. My first thought was the bird somehow fell off of the upper level where all the bird feeders were and the bird broke its wing. I went and got some toilet paper to pick the bird up. I thought it was dying and I didn't want either of our two retrievers to find it.

As I picked up the bird in my hands, I was stunned to see the bird was all tangled and entwined with fishing line all around its legs and its body. Instinctively, I started talking to the bird like it could hear me clearly and understand me. I told it it would be alright;

that I would untangle the fishing line and set it free. I even stroked the back of its neck. The bird was obviously scared and knew it was bound and couldn't get free by itself. I gently unwound the fishing line from around its body. I then walked down off the porch and put the bird in the grass and told it, it was free and to fly back to the tree by the porch to be safe. As I walked back on the porch, I looked back and it wasn't moving. Then I thought a neighbor cat could get it or even our dogs and this bird had to still be in shock or dying since it won't move. Going back down, I talked to the bird, reassuring it it was now—free from being all tangled and bound up. Then I noticed its eyes began to blink, so I turned and went back in the house feeling it would be alright. I left the door open about six inches while I went to get my suitcases and some more toilet paper in case I needed to take the bird upstairs where the bird feeder was on the porch.

When I went back to see if it needed to be put upstairs so other animals wouldn't get it, both my dogs went bounding out the door. They used their snouts to push the door open enough for them to get through. My instinct kicked in and I just said to the dogs loudly, "Stop! heel!" I was shocked to see them freeze, looking down at the bird.

I then said, "Come." I was on the porch, and they came. Training them since they were pups really paid off. I put them back in the house and closed the door. I then turned around and talked very gentle to the bird from the porch. "It is alright, wee one. You are just fine now." The bird looked up at me, then flew up into the evergreen tree next to the porch and just stayed perched there, looking at me for some time as if she was saying "Thank you."

At this point, I remembered that even the birds are taken care of by God, as is pointed out in the Bible.

I began to reflect on the parallels between the way that little bird was bound up by fishing line and how Lazarus was bound up by grave clothes. Jesus said to the people when Lazarus came out of the grave with his hands and feet wrapped with Strips of linen and a cloth around his face, "Take off the grave clothes and let him go." (John 11:44) We are called by faith and the Holy Spirit, guidance to release people from the things that bind them as they experience freedom in Christ.

Chapter 15

The Shepherd's Mark

"When Walid Shoebat, author of Obsession, spoke at the National Wildlife Museum in Jackson Hole, Wyoming, I met with him and his wife before he spoke. Shoebat, an Arab converted to Christianity, supports Israel and he has an awesome testimony. As I spoke with his wife, she asked if I could pray for their lives. I felt led by the Holy Spirit to give her my necklace; it was the Shepherd's Mark. I told her that I, and others who have this necklace, would be praying for Israel, for all those who love and support the Jewish people, and for those like them, who are on the frontlines." (Patty Atkins).

In the 1970s, while living in Miami, Florida, I had the privilege of creating, coordinating, and leading a citywide prayer rally sponsored by Campus Crusade for Christ International, now known as

CRU International. I was amazed at how everything went together. I couldn't explain it; God did it supernaturally.

My chosen speaker, Corrie ten Boom, was available for the date we wanted. The plan we were given by the Holy Spirit came together in the height of the tourist season. The place we were prompted to use was booked, but when the Jewish manager learned that the speaker was from a family who hid Jews during the Holocaust, a cancellation just *happened* to open for the very date I had requested.

The prayer rally was packed. The testimonies were incredible and considered a major success. Prayer groups were created in many neighborhoods, schools, police and fire departments, and even on the Air Force base. Prayer chains were formed because of the supernatural answers to prayer. When this began happening in Miami, prayer moved nationwide. Prayer workshops were developed and taught. The unity being created among the Christians in Miami stood out. Representatives from each denomination came together to form an accountability group for all of us who were in leadership.

This is when I received the vision of the Shepherd's Mark. I didn't know then what all the parts of the symbol meant, except that I knew the triangle represented the Trinity—God the Father, God the Son, and God the Holy Spirit. I remembered that the early Christians had used a fish as a means of identification, as well as a form of communication. But I thought that God was showing me a purpose that was something more than a way to communicate. The vision was not only of the Triune Godhead, but a symbol of the unity we were witnessing in Miami; a unity that God wants to see among all His people.

When I realized this, I called one of the accountability representatives—the southern district superintendent of schools in Miami. I told him about the vision I had received. I asked him not to laugh at me as I described the picture I was seeing and asked if he could recommend an artist who could draw a replica of my vision. He found a young substitute teacher who agreed to help me. Within two hours, he handed me the drawing with his blessings. He had drawn exactly what I saw and told me he was a Christian brother. I told him I would continue to ask the Holy Spirit to guide me until the use of the vision was fulfilled for the body of Christ.

As I continued to work in prayer ministry and teaching prayer and evangelistic workshops, I watched the tremendous moving of the Holy Spirit in Florida. I kept waiting on Him to guide me; I asked Him to tell me what to do with the emblem that I had made into a piece of jewelry. Then one morning while my husband was praying, the Holy Spirit spoke to him and told him we were to move to the North Carolina mountains. After moving to North Carolina, I continued to teach workshops, keeping the same theme the previous workshops had, which was *to teach you to teach others.*

Although I had not planned to look for another job, the local hospital was looking for an x-ray technologist, and inner promptings continuously nudged me to apply. I brought my skills back up to date, applied, and was hired. I had been working there almost a year when, one evening, after working all day, I was called back in at 11:00 p.m. There had been a horrendous accident related to alcohol. I had finished with the last patient at 2:00 a.m. and was headed home when I started praying from deep within my soul. I simply prayed, "Jesus, is this what You want me to do for the rest of my life? I know You put in my heart the desire to have You work through me in outreach and teaching. Please speak to me." When He spoke my name, I was so startled I almost ran off the road!

The Holy Spirit then started to speak words from the Bible to me. After getting home, I got my Bible and concordance and started writing down what I had heard. I really didn't know where these verses were in the Bible, but I didn't want to forget what He spoke.

"Commit your way to the Lord Trudy, trust also in Him, and He shall bring it to pass" (Psalm 37:5).

"I will instruct and teach you in the way you shall go, I will guide you with my eye upon you" (Psalm 32:8).

"Your ears will hear a word behind you, "This is the way, walk in it," whenever you turn to the right or the left" (Isaiah 30:21).

"If you lack wisdom, ask of God, who gives to all men generously and without reproach, and it will be given to him. Ask in faith, without doubting" (James 1:5, 1:6).

"Call unto Me, and I will answer and show you great and mighty things, which you don't know" (Jeremiah 33:3).

The verses are quoted exactly the way I remembered them at that time. I wanted directions to follow next. Before I left Florida, a couple of names were suggested for what to call this emblem. One was FOCUS: Followers of Christ United Spiritually. The other name was the *Shepherd's Mark*.

As I continued to pray and wait on the Holy Spirit to instruct me, a few girls' names were put on my mind, so I contacted them. I told them what was going on and asked if we could meet. We did, and within two hours, an organizational plan came together. An International Crisis Prayer Network (ICPN) was created around the United States for connecting the lead intercessors of twenty-five ministries to one another. We would use the Shepherd's Mark emblem with the ICPN Ministry until we found its final purpose. Pam Spears wrote a song titled "Make Us One Heart."

I kept being prompted to find a deeper meaning to the Shepherd's Mark because of the flames. At a conference in North Carolina, after a Hebrew scholar spoke on the unity between the Father, the Son, and the Holy Spirit, I showed him the emblem. I asked if he knew what it meant, and he said, "Yes, I will send the meaning to you." This was his following response:

> The emblem merges images into a graceful, yet awe-inspiring symbol. One triangle signifies the trinity of God reaching down, the divine presence being superimposed on the trinity of man: body, soul, and spirit. But the focus is God, not man: the fire reveals the Father, with the bold declaration, 'Our God is a consuming fire;' the Son in the cross, through which Jesus brought redemption to man; and the Holy Spirit in the dove, a symbol of God's peace which surpasses all understanding. Together the three bring life and peace to all believers. The Shepherd's Mark demonstrates the power of God's grace manifest in the hearts of His people as they unite their spirits with Him in prayer and worship. (John D. Garr, PhD, Th.D. Atlanta, Georgia)

Many years later, my close friend Beverly Castetter did an in-depth study of both the Old and New Testaments concerning the seven parts that make up the Shepherd's Mark. Each part has a meaning; together, they are a sacred symbol of biblical truth.

(1) The Two Triangles: The upward pointing triangle depicts the mind, body, and soul of man attempting to reach God. The downward pointing triangle, covered in flames and water, represents the Triune God reaching down to man through Jesus, the Messiah. The Old and New Testaments reveal God's attempts to get the attention of the Jewish people. Though they clung to God Himself, most of them refused to see Jesus as the Messiah. Then God turned to the Gentiles to spread His message so that the Jews—and all people—might know the remaining two persons of the Trinity: Jesus and the Holy Spirit.

"A Father of the fatherless, a defender of widows, is God in His holy habitation" (Psalm 68:5).

"For unto us a Child is born, unto us a Son is given; and the government will be upon His shoulders. And His name will be called Wonderful, Counselor, Mighty God, Everlasting Father, Prince of Peace" (Isaiah 9:6).

"But you shall receive power when the Holy Spirit has come upon you" (Acts 1:8).

(2) The Cross: In the center of the circle within the two triangles is the cross upon which Jesus died to bring deliverance from sin's penalty. Jesus Christ paid the price so that the believer could be freed from sin to spend eternity in God's presence. The cross reminds us of God's great grace which reached down to bridge the chasm between Himself and sinful man through the death of His Son. Thus showing His immeasurable love for us so that we might have eternal life.

"Men of Israel, hear these words: Jesus of Nazareth, a Man attested by God to you, by miracles, wonders, and signs which God did through Him in your midst, as you yourselves also know—Him, being delivered by the determined purpose and foreknowledge of God, you have taken by lawless hands, have crucified, and put to death; whom God raised up, having loosed the pains of death, because it was not possible that He should be held by it" (Acts 2:22–24).

"For God so loved the world that He gave His only begotten Son, that whoever believes in Him should not perish, but have everlasting life" (John 3:16).

(3) The Circle: A symbol of eternity. The circle around the cross and the dove represents the eternal and complete God. Just as there is no beginning and no end with a circle, there is no beginning or end with God. When we accept Jesus as our Savior, God welcomes us into His eternity. He gives us a new beginning and the promise that He will be with us forever. Similar to the wedding ring and the marriage covenant, it symbolizes an intimate personal relationship with Christ.

"'I am the Alpha and the Omega, the Beginning and the End,' says the Lord, 'who is and who was and who is to come, the Almighty'" (Revelation 1:8).

"Being confident of this very thing, that He who has begun a good work in you will complete it until the day of Jesus Christ" (Philippians 1:6).

"For the Lord Himself will descend from heaven with a shout, with the voice of an archangel, and with the trumpet of God… Then we who are alive and remain shall be caught up…in the clouds to meet the Lord in the air. And thus we shall always be with the Lord" (1 Thessalonians 4:16, 4:17).

(4) The Flames: Two-thirds of the gold triangle is covered with flames, representing the cleansing power of fire, as God the Father reaches down to purify us. In the Old Testament, fire was used for sacrificing, destroying, burning, devouring, attracting attention, being a light, and protecting. In the New Testament, fire demonstrates the purifying that God does in our lives through His Spirit so He can live through us.

"I indeed baptize you with water unto repentance, but He who is coming after me is mightier than I, whose sandals I am not worthy to carry. He will baptize you with the Holy Spirit and fire" (Matthew 3:11).

"So God, who knows the heart, acknowledged them by giving them the Holy Spirit, just as He did to us, and made no distinction between us and them, purifying their hearts by faith" (Acts 15:8, 15:9).

"For our God is a consuming fire" (Hebrews 12:29).

(5) The Water: The lower third of the gold triangle is covered with water, which represents both the baptism that washes away our sins, and the fact that Jesus is the wellspring of living water. Once we are cleansed, His living water flows through us. Only His living water can truly quench our thirsty souls.

"If you knew the gift of God, and who it is who says to you, 'Give Me a drink,' you would have asked Him, and He would have given you living water" (John 4:10).

"He who believes in Me, as the Scripture has said, out of his heart will flow rivers of living water" (John 7:8).

"Then Peter said to them, 'Repent, and let every one of you be baptized in the name of Jesus Christ for the remission of sins; and you shall receive the gift of the Holy Spirit'" (Acts 2:38).

"For the Lamb who is in the midst of the throne will shepherd them and lead them to living fountains of waters" (Revelation 7:17).

(6) The Dove and His Eye: At the center of the cross is the dove representing the Holy Spirit. God's Spirit is a person, not a thing. He joins with our spirit the moment we personally accept Jesus Christ as Savior and Lord. When Jesus ascended to heaven after His resurrection, God did not leave us without a comforter or helper, but sent His Spirit as an advantage to empower us. The Holy Spirit sends people out to do what Jesus wants them to do. He forbids certain actions and intercedes for us. He teaches, testifies, convicts of sin, guides into truth, inspires scripture, and speaks to us. While the dove represents the Holy Spirit, the eye of the dove is important in its own right. The eye is a symbol of the personal care with which the Holy Spirit guides every believer individually. With unwavering focus, God continually watches over His children.

"When He had been baptized, Jesus came up immediately from the water; and behold, the heavens were opened to Him, and He saw the Spirit of God descending like a dove and alighting upon Him" (Matthew 3:16).

"And I will pray the Father, and He will give you another Helper, that He may abide with you forever—the Spirit of truth, whom the world cannot receive, because it neither sees Him nor knows Him; but you know Him, for He dwells with you and will be in you" (John 14:16, 14:17).

"Nevertheless, I tell you the truth. It is to your advantage that I go away; for if I do not go away, the Helper will not come to you; but if I depart, I will send Him to you" (John 16:7).

"Likewise, the Spirit also helps in our weaknesses. For we do not know what we should pray for as we ought, but the Spirit Himself makes intercession for us with groanings which cannot be uttered" (Romans 8:26).

"For the eyes of the Lord run to and fro throughout the whole earth, to show Himself strong on behalf of those whose heart is loyal to Him" (2 Chronicles 16:9).

"I will instruct you and teach you in the way you should go; I will guide you with My eye" (Psalm 32:8).

(7) The Star of David: The combined triangles in this emblem form the Star of David, the historic symbol of Judaism. As unusual as it may seem for Christians to wear the Star of David, it is a beautiful reminder of our history. Jesus Christ, our Savior and Redeemer, was "the son of David" (Matthew 1:1). Indeed, the earthly lineage of Jesus is recorded through forty-two generations back to Abraham, the father of the Jewish people. In this emblem, the Star of David reminds us of our shared history and reminds Christians and Jews alike to pray for the peace of Jerusalem, as we are instructed to do.

> "Pray for the peace of Jerusalem: 'May they prosper who love you'" (Psalm 122:6).

> "I will bless those who bless [Israel], and I will curse him who curses [Israel]" (Genesis 12:3).

"For thus says the Lord of hosts: He sent Me after glory, to the nations which plunder you; for he who touches you touches the apple of His eye" (Zechariah 2:8).

By the time Bev had helped me to define these different parts, my husband Hub and I were well established in North Carolina. I began earnestly seeking the purpose behind the Shepherd's Mark. Hub was an avid supporter and encouraged me even when he became terminally ill. After his death, my daughter Carolyn was a tremendous support, both in my grieving process and encouraging me to continue my work with the Shepherd's Mark. We developed a companion booklet to go with the necklace and had it copywritten. After attempting a sole proprietorship, I felt having a board and partners was important, so we formed an LLC. The symbol was trademarked, and necklace sales began to increase.

Many of those who wear the necklace have told me stories of how it acts almost like a magnet, attracting opportunities to share the meaning with anyone interested, and therefore allows you to spread the good news of salvation! God began to reveal that this ability to witness, just by sharing the meaning behind the Shepherd's Mark, was an important part of its purpose. By studying the meaning of each part of this sacred symbol, you can be ready to answer questions. We can assure inquirers of Jesus's promise to always be with them (Matthew 28:20) by inviting them to pray:

"Dear Jesus,
"I know I've made mistakes and that makes me a sinner, but I believe You died for my sins and miraculously rose from the dead. I'm asking You to forgive me and to come into my life. I want a personal relationship with You. I'm committing to trust and follow You as my Lord and Savior.

"In Your name I pray,
Amen."

It was also during Hub's illness that I met Larry Stamm, a messianic Jew who was teaching at a church near my daughter's in Tennessee. He commented about how he thought the Shepherd's Mark was such *a beautiful piece of jewelry!* He told me that he thought it was *a wonderful symbol of the peace of God found in the Holy One of Israel, Messiah Jesus.* It was through his teachings, and especially through my continued friendship with Corrie ten Boom over the years, that I began to realize the Triune purpose behind this sacred symbol.

These were not the only ones who encouraged me throughout the process, though. There were important people who I developed lasting friendships with along the way. Billy Graham made a movie about Corrie's life, and one of the board members for *The Hiding Place* was Mike Atkins, the senior pastor at the Chapel at River Crossing in Jackson Hole, Wyoming. He shared with me that he felt "the Shepherd's Mark, in addition to being a beautifully designed work of art, serves an important function in reminding its owner to be in regular and sincere prayer for the peace of Jerusalem and for the unfolding plans and purposes of God in human history." Once again, God was revealing His purpose for the Shepherd's Mark. Mike and his wife Patty remain good friends and are now serving on the Shepherd's Mark Board.

My own pastor, Gary Hewins, at Community Bible Church, commented that "this one-of-a-kind Shepherd's Mark pleases the eye and draws attention to two realities—worn close to the heart, the Shepherd's Mark reminds us to pray for the peace of Jerusalem while we share the power of the gospel in word and in deed." Repeatedly, God revealed this Triune purpose!

By now, you must be wondering what this threefold purpose is. But first, I want to remind you of something I mentioned in my introduction. I was a baby Christian, and as I met people along the way, like Vonette Bright who cofounded Campus Crusade for Christ, now CRU, I simply enjoyed fellowship with them and thought nothing about becoming good friends. It wasn't until much later that I realized how important these people were. After the Miami Prayer Rally and forming ICPN Ministries, Vonette continued to encourage me. Through this process, after I moved to North Carolina, I began serving at The Cove on their prayer ministry team. There, I became friends with Gigi, Billy Graham's oldest daughter. Again, I thought nothing of my fellowship with these women, and even though I had matured in my Christian walk, I still didn't realize how important these women were.

I want to share one more encouragement that I received from Russ Carroll. You might recognize his name because he was the lead financial coach for The Dave Ramsey Show for many years before his retirement. He now serves as a financial consultant for Focus on the Family's radio program. Russ helped me navigate my finances after Hub died, and he and I became fast friends. We are kindred spirits because we both have a heart for the Jews. He also agreed to join our board and asserts that *the world will be convinced Jesus came from the Father by our unity amid diversity.* The Shepherd's Mark clearly identifies that those who follow the Shepherd of our souls—Jew and Gentile believers alike—can burn brightly with the Light that can ignite the hearts of all who will look to Him for hope and forgiveness.

Like Russ, many of these friends and encouragers became board members of the Shepherd's Mark. Those who have partnered with me in the LLC take on the lion's share of the work, but we couldn't do it without the valuable advice that the board provides. One thing several of our board members brought to our attention is the need to support other ministries with any profits. Although we are not a nonprofit, the ministries we support are. Again, with the Holy Spirit's guidance, we were led to support a ministry that reflects our values. One that was a grass roots ministry in Israel and had been thoroughly vetted through organizations like Charisma magazine, the Evangelical Council for Financial Accountability (ECFA) and Nonprofit Analytics. Even CRU and Chosen People Ministries support One for Israel, the grass roots ministry that we chose. They are based in Netanya, Israel.

One For Israel's website states, we "understand that there are many ways to bless Israel, but we are convinced that the best way to bless Israel is with Yeshua the Messiah (Jesus Christ)." They seek to fulfill this by reaching Israelis with the gospel message, but their media evangelism exceeds well beyond their borders. Joel Rosenburg, in his recent interview with Greg Laurie, stated that "some young people, who loved the Lord, realized, by Google analytics, that 100,000 times a month, Hebrew seekers were googling 'Who is the Messiah?'" One for Israel's media evangelism "was established in 2009 with the encouragement of Campus Crusade for Christ." However, they also serve the humanitarian needs that many other ministries strive to meet. Given that their Bible college and media outreach are thoroughly vetted, they can coordinate this aid "with the city municipality to find households in great need, particularly Jewish Holocaust survivors, and to take them gifts of food and supplies." Most importantly, they are "training up the next generation of leaders [through]…the only accredited Hebrew-speaking seminary in the world!" They are also "the only Hebrew-speaking messianic Bible college in Israel." One For Israel was the obvious choice to begin with given the Triune purpose of the Shepherd's Mark.

Go to this page to watch videos of their quality work: https://www.oneforisrael.org/category/bible-based-teachinu-from-israel/video/

So here it is. Our prayer is that the Shepherd's Mark will fulfill the following threefold purpose:

(1) A constant reminder for both Christians and Jews to pray for Jerusalem;

"Pray for the peace of Jerusalem, they shall prosper that love thee" (Psalm 122:6).

"I will bless those who bless you, and I will curse him who curses you" (Genesis 12:3).

(2) An evangelistic emblem to visually portray the unity of the body of Christ that Jesus prayed for in John 17:20–23. The unity of both Old and New Testament believers is represented though the two triangles. The Trinity of the Old Testament is pointing up, symbolizing man's attempt to reach God; the Trinity of the New Testament is superimposed over it and pointing down, displaying God's great love through Christ.

Each component of the Shepherd's Mark is a witnessing tool to share God's love; and

(3) A source of provision for ministries that the Shepherd's Mark Board of Advisors determines to qualify by way of guidance from the Holy Spirit, fervent prayer, and thorough research.

"The Shepherd's Mark is truly a remarkable and powerful symbol; I have trouble calling it jewelry. There is no other image that better symbolizes God's love for us than that of the Shepherd. Every time I see this beautiful symbol, I am reminded that Jesus is my Shepherd and the keeper of my soul."

—David Spears
Retired Chairman, Club Management Associates
Full Time Follower of the Good Shepherd
Current Shepherd's Mark Board Chairman

If you are interested in learning more about the Shepherd's Mark or ordering one for yourself or others, please visit our website at www.shepherdsmark.com.

About the Author

Trudy Sherry was thirty-five when she was introduced to Jesus Christ.

Born in Brooklyn and raised by a family that had no religious beliefs, she searched for meaning in sports, a medical career, marriage, and Communism. None of them brought fulfillment.

A miraculous healing of her son and the death of her twin boys sent her looking for the meaning in life. A seventeen-year-old electrical apprentice challenged her to learn more about the life-changing difference that Jesus could make. Her life has never been the same.

Through simple story telling, no less than 1,000 people have come to know faith in Jesus and the hope believing in Him can bring.

Join us for a story of faith, simplicity, and hope. Let us introduce you to this Man that she thought was a swear word.

CPSIA information can be obtained
at www.ICGtesting.com
Printed in the USA
LVHW052347210920
666746LV00002BA/450